OUR AUSTRALASIAN STORY

This edition published 2017
By Living Book Press
147 Durren Rd, Jilliby, 2259

Copyright © Living Book Press, 2017

ISBN: 9781925729177

A catalogue record for this
book is available from the
National Library of Australia

Our Australasian Story

Stories of Australia and New Zealand

Told to Children by H.E. MARSHALL
With pictures by J. R. SKELTON

AUSTRALIA

NEW ZEALAND

ABOUT THIS BOOK

"The Empire upon which the sun never sets." We all know these words, and we say them with a somewhat proud and grand air, for that vast Empire is ours. It belongs to us, and we to it.

But although we are proud of our Empire it may be that some of us know little of its history. We only know it as it now is, and we forget perhaps that there was a time when it did not exist. We forget that it has grown to be great out of very small beginnings. We forget that it did not grow great all at once, but that with pluck and patience our fellow-countrymen built it up by little and by little, each leaving behind him a vaster inheritance than he found. So, "lest we forget," in this book I have told a few of the most exciting and interesting stories about the building up of this our great heritage and possession.

But we cannot

> "Rise with the sun and ride with the same,
> Until the next morning he rises again."

We cannot in one day grid the whole world about, following the sun in his course, visiting with him all the many countries, all the scattered islands of the sea which form the mighty Empire upon which he never ceases to shine. No, it will take us many days to compass the journey, and little eyes would ache, little brains be weary long before the tale ended did I try to tell of all "the far-away isles of home, where the old speech is native, and the old flag floats." So in this book you will find stories of five of the five chief portions of our Empire only, that of Canada, Australia, New Zealand, South Africa, and India.[1] But perhaps some day, if you greet these stories as kindly as you have greeted those of England and of Scotland, I will tell you in another book more stories of Our Empire.

The stories are not all bright. How should they be? We have made mistakes, we have been checked here, we have stumbled there. We may own it without shame, perhaps almost without sorrow, and still love our Empire and its builders. Still we may say,

> "Where shall the watchful sun,
>   England, my England,
> Match the master-work you've done,
>   England, my own?
> When shall we rejoice agen
> Such a breed of mighty men
> As come forward, one to ten,
>   To the song on your bugles blown,
>   England—
> Down the years on your bugles blown?"

H.E. MARSHALL

Oxford, 1908

---

1. This collection only includes the sections featuring Australia and New Zealand.

AUSTRALIA

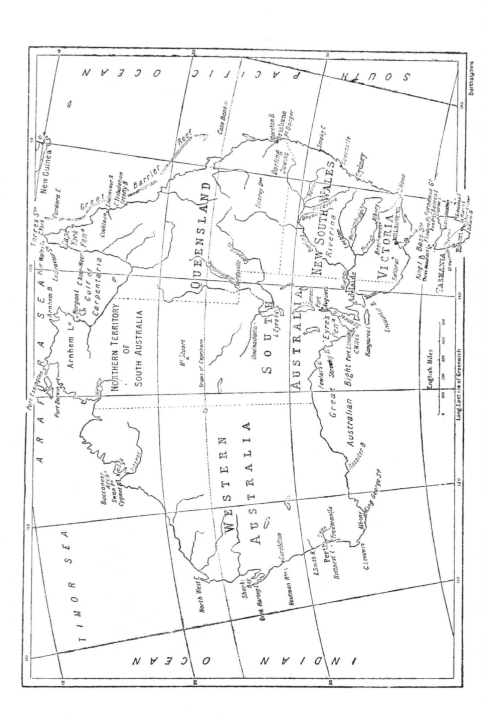

CHAPTER I

"THERE IS NOTHING NEW UNDER THE SUN"

W ISE people tell us that the land of Australia is perhaps the oldest in the world. At a time when the wide ocean swept over the continent of Europe, when our little island still lay far beneath the rippling waves, the land of Australia stood above the lone waters.

Yet to us Australia is a new discovered country. Long ages ago indeed travellers and learned men told tales of a Great South Land which lay somewhere in the Southern Seas. But no eye had seen that fabled country, no ship had touched that unknown shore. It was a country dim and mysterious as fairyland. On ancient maps we find it marked with rough uncertain lines, "The Southerne Unknowne Lande," but how it came to be so marked, how the stories about it first came to be told, and believed, we shall very likely never know.

It is hard to tell too, who, among white men, first set foot on this great island. If one of the brave sailors of those far-off times did by chance touch upon its shore, he found little there to make him stay, or encourage him to return. For in those days what men chiefly sought was trade. And in Australia there was no place for trade. It was a great, wide, silent land where there were no towns, or even houses. It was peopled only by a few black savages, who wore no clothes, who had no wants, and who cared for nothing but to eat and drink.

But in the seventeenth century, when Holland was mistress of the seas, and the Dutch planted their flag on every shore, they found their way to the Great South Land.

It was a Dutchman who discovered Tasmania. He called it Van Dieman's Land in honour of the Governor-General of the Dutch East Indies. But the name was afterwards changed to Tasmania, by which name we know it now. The great Gulf of Carpentaria is named after another Dutchman, and all round the northern, western and southern shores, here and there may be found names to remind us of those old Dutch adventurers. But the name New Holland which the Dutch gave to the whole land has long since been forgotten.

The Dutch did little more than discover the coast. They founded no colonies, they built no towns, and so their hold on the land was hardly real. They marked New Holland upon their maps, but they knew little about it. No man knew what a vast land New Holland was, or how far stretching were the rolling plains of which they had had only a glimpse.

Soon Holland as a great sea power gave way to another which was to become still greater. Van Tromp the Dutchman was beaten by Blake the Englishman. And after that the Dutch seem to have lost all interest in the Great South Land.

Then in 1699 a British sailor called Dampier set out on a voyage of discovery to the Southern seas. He was more than half a pirate and had led a life of wild adventure. But he was a daring seaman, and had already been to New Holland more than once. And so King William III. chose him to lead an expedition of discovery.

One February day Dampier sailed out from England, and six months later anchored in a bay on the west coast of New Holland, which he called Shark's Bay, because his men killed and ate many sharks there. It is still called Shark's Bay.

For some time Dampier cruised along the shores taking note of all that he saw, of the land, the birds, and beasts. Among the birds, Dampier saw gaily coloured parrots and cockatoos, and black swans. Among the beasts, the chief was a curious-looking animal with a long tail and long hind legs upon which it leaped and hopped about. The natives called it Kanguro.

He saw a few natives. They were tall, thin, and black, with blinking eyes and frizzled hair. They had no weapons except wooden spears, they wore no clothes, and their houses, which he only saw in the distance, looked to him like haycocks. But some had no houses at all. "They lay in the open air without covering, the earth being their bed and heaven their canopy. They had no possessions of any kind. Not soe much as a catt or a dog." With such people there was no hope of trade, and in those days no one thought of taking possession of a land unless there was some trade to be done.

Having cruised about for some time and finding no fresh water, Dampier feared to stay longer, lest his men should fall ill in that desert land. So he steered away to the East Indies and from thence sailed homeward.

Many years passed. Now and again a ship touched upon the shores of New Holland but no one took much interest in it. It was a barren, useless land most men thought, a stony desert for the greater part, good enough for the few wild black fellows who lived there, but never a home for white men. Besides this, the British, who were now the great sea power, were busy fighting in India and America, and had little time and few ships to spare for peaceful exploration.

But in the long reign of George III. , when after much fighting Britain was at length at peace with all the world, men once more turned their thoughts to peaceful things. Then in 1768 Captain James Cook was sent upon an exploring expedition.

James Cook had had a very exciting life, but there is no room to tell about it here. As a small boy he was sent to serve in a draper's shop, but at the age of fourteen he ran away to sea, and from then till now when he was forty, his life had been full of excitement and adventure.

In this voyage, Captain Cook sailed all along the eastern coast of Australia, a thing which no white man had ever done. He landed in many places, naming capes, bays, and points, as he passed. One great bay he named Botany Bay, because of the many plants and flowers to be found there. And here he set up the Union Jack, cut the name of his ship and the date of his landing on the trees near, and claimed the land for King George.

Cook and his men had many adventures. At one time they were nearly wrecked. The ship struck upon a rock and stuck fast. The water began to come in so quickly, that although the men worked hard at the pumps, it seemed as if the ship would sink. But luckily the sea was smooth, and there was little wind, and after much hard work they were able to steer into a safe harbour. Here they ran the ship ashore, and found a hole in the bottom big enough to have sunk it. But by good fortune a piece of coral rock had stuck in the hole, and this had saved them.

Having mended the ship as best they could they once more set sail, and at last readied what is now known as Torres Strait, having explored the whole eastern coast of Australia.

At Torres Strait Cook landed. Once more he set up the British flag and claimed the whole eastern coast with all its bays, harbours, rivers, and islands, for King George. And to this great tract he gave the name of New South Wales. There in that far-off land, their little ship, a mere speck between blue sky and bluer sea, this handful of Britons claimed new realms for their king. And to attest their claim, volley upon volley of musketry rolled out, awakening the deep silence of that unknown shore. There was none to answer or deny the challenge, and when the noise of cannon died upon the quiet air there was only the sigh of trees, the ripple of waves, and the scream of wild birds to break the stillness.

CHAPTER II

THE FOUNDING OF SYDNEY

A FTER Cook sailed away the great island-continent was left once again to silent loneliness. Cook made other voyages, but did not discover much more of Australia, and for many years few white men touched upon the shores of the Great South Land.

Then came the war in which Britain lost all her American colonies. It was a great loss, how great at the time perhaps few knew. But in one way the loss soon began to be felt.

The British in those days instead of keeping evil-doers in prison at home, used to send them to work upon the farms or plantations in America. When America was no longer a part of the British Empire, convicts, as such evil-doers were called, could not be sent there. The prisons at home became full to overflowing. Something had to be done, and at last it was decided to make use of New South Wales and found a colony there to which convicts might be sent.

So on 13th May 1787, the "First Fleet," as it afterwards came to be called by Australians, sailed out on its long voyage. In the eight or ten ships there were about a thousand people. Nearly eight hundred of these were convicts, both men and women, the rest were soldiers and marines to guard them.

With the fleet, as Governor-General of the new colony, went Captain Arthur Phillip.

On the way out the ships stopped at Teneriffe and at Cape Town, where the Dutch Governor received them kindly. Here they took aboard so many cocks and hens, sheep and cattle, that the ships looked more like Noah's arks than anything else.

In June 1788 the new colonists arrived at Botany Bay, where it had been decided to found the colony. But Captain Phillip did not think it a good place, and went exploring in a small boat further north until he found the beautiful Jackson Bay.

Here Captain Phillip decided to found the new colony. He landed and set up the Union Jack, and gathering round the flagstaff, he and his officers drank to the king's health, and to the success of the colony.

The convicts were landed, the soldiers were drawn up in line, guns were fired, and Captain Phillip made a speech to the convicts. He told them that now under a new sky, in a new home, they had once again a chance to forget their evil ways, and begin a new life. Once again they had a chance to prove themselves good British subjects. This was the first speech in the English language that had ever been made in that far-off land, and when Captain Phillip had finished, a British cheer rang out.

Thus the city of Sydney was founded.

Now began a busy time. The stillness of that silent land was broken for ever. All day long the woods rang with the sound of the axe. All day long the ring of hammer and anvil was heard, the tinkle of the mason's trowel, the sighing of the carpenter's saw. There was everything to do. There were houses to build, roads to cut, harbours to make. The land had first to be cleared of trees, and wood and stone had to be quarried and hewn for building. With all this to do, there was little time left for farming.

Besides, among the soldiers, and sailors, and convicts, there were no farmers. None among them knew how to set about the work. The season was dry, the seed which was sown did not sprout, or was eaten by rats, and there was little or no harvest.

The sheep and cattle died, or ran away into the forest and were seen no more.

Soon the food which had been brought from home grew scarce, and the promised ships which were to bring more, did not appear. The little colony began to starve. Convicts and freemen alike grew gaunt and pale. The governor himself knew what it meant to go hungry, for he would not fare better than the others, and he gave up his private stores for the use of all. "If any convict complains," he said, "let him come to Government House, and he will see that we are no better off there."

Hollow-cheeked and faint, every man looked eagerly, longingly, out to sea, straining weary eyes to catch a glimpse of a white sail upon the blue waste of water. Day after day passed. No sail appeared. Little work was done, for men who are always hungry cannot work.

The colonists had brought food for two years. Now three had passed, and still no help came from home. With hundreds and hundreds of miles between them and Britain, they seemed to be cast away and forgotten. They knew nothing of what was happening in the world. They had no means of knowing if they were really forgotten, or if some mischance had befallen the ships sent out to them. There was no way by which they could send a message home. They could do nothing but wait.

At last one morning a ship came in sight What joy there was! The women wept, the men cheered.

Eagerly the colonists crowded round the new arrivals asking for news of home. They heard with joy that they had not been utterly forgotten and neglected. Ships with stores had been sent, but had been wrecked on the way.

Soon another ship arrived, then another and another, The long pain of hunger was at an end, and for a time at least the little colony was saved from starvation. But famine came upon them again, and at one time things were so bad that people who were asked to dine at Government House were told to bring their own bread with them.

With the ships bringing food to the colony came a regiment of soldiers. They were called the New South Wales Corps. The Marines and their officers, who had come out in the "First Fleet," then went home; and Captain Phillip was not sorry that they should go, for although they had been sent out to help to keep the convicts in order, they had themselves been very unruly, and had added much to the governor's difficulties. These difficulties were great, for it was no easy matter to rule a colony made up of wild, bad men, sent there in punishment of their misdeeds. But, as will be seen, the New South Wales Corps was not much help to the governor.

In December 1792 Governor Phillip, worn out by five years of hardship, gave up his post and sailed home.

He was succeeded by Captain Hunter, but until he arrived the colony was left in the hands of Major Grose, leader of the New South Wales Corps.

Captain Phillip had been gentle and just. He had shared every hardship with the colonists, and had tried to make the convicts better. Grose cared nothing for the improvement of the convicts, and he was utterly unfit to rule. He allowed the soldiers to do as they liked, and they very soon became wild, riotous, and drunken. They took everything into their own hands, and soon from being merely soldiers, they became the merchants and rulers of the colony. Everything coming into the colony had to pass through their hands. But the thing they traded in most, and made most money out of, was rum.

Some free settlers had now come to Sydney, and they were allowed to have convicts to help them on their farms. The officers and men of the New South Wales Corps also took land, and had convict labourers, whom they paid for their work in rum. The soldiers made friends of these convicts, and they drank and gambled together, so that the convicts, instead of becoming better, became worse, and when Governor Hunter arrived, he found that all the good that Governor Phillip had done was destroyed. The whole colony was filled with riot, disorder, drunkenness, and misery.

Captain Hunter tried to put things right again. He tried to stop the trade in rum, but he was not strong enough to do it. The "Rum Corps," as the soldiers came to be called, had got the upper hand, and they meant to keep it. So during the whole time of Hunter's rule, he had to fight the men and officers of the Rum Corps.

This was the darkest time in the whole history of Australia. But dark though it was, it was now that the foundation of Australia's greatness in trade was laid.

With the New South Wales Corps there had come out a Captain John MacArthur. He, like so many others, received a grant of land, and began farming. He soon saw that the land was very good for rearing sheep, and began to turn his attention to them. But whereas others thought of rearing them for food, he thought of them for their wool. After a great deal of trouble he got "wool-bearing sheep," first from the Cape, and then from King George's own famous flock of Spanish merino sheep.

At this time the British got most of the wool they needed for their great factories from Spain. But Napoleon, who was fighting Britain in every way possible, now tried to ruin their trade by forbidding all the people of Europe to trade with them. When they could no longer get wool from Spain, the British wool trade began to suffer. Then it was that MacArthur stepped in. From his sheep-farm he was soon able to send shiploads of wool to the factories at home, thus preventing the ruin of British manufactures, and bringing wealth to Australia. From then till now the industry has grown, and now millions of pounds' worth of wool are exported every year.

CHAPTER III

THE ADVENTURES OF GEORGE BASS AND
MATTHEW FLINDERS

"See! girt with tempest and wing'd with thunder,
And clad with lightning and shod with sleet,
The strong waves treading the swift waves, sunder
The flying rollers with frothy feet.
One gleam like a blood-shot sword swims on
The skyline, staining the green gulf crimson,
A death stroke fiercely dealt by a dim sun,
That strikes through his stormy winding-sheet.

Oh! brave white horses! you gather and gallop,
The storm sprite loosens the gusty reins;
Now the stoutest ship were the frailest shallop
In your hollow backs, on your high arched manes."

A. LINDSAY GORDON.

IT was not until the town of Sydney had been founded for
some years that anything was known of the great island upon
which it was built. But at last people became curious to know
more about their new home.

When Captain John Hunter came out from home as Governor of New South Wales, there came with him two daring
young men. The one was George Bass, the ship's doctor, and

"NATIVES GATHERED ROUND THEM."

the other Matthew Flinders, a midshipman. Flinders was only twenty-one, and Bass a few years older.

These two soon became fast friends. They both were eager to know more of the land to which they had come, and about a month after they arrived in Sydney, they set out on a voyage of discovery in a little boat of eight feet long. They called it the Tom Thumb, and the whole crew was themselves and a boy.

In this tiny boat they sailed out into the great Pacific, and made for Botany Bay. Here they cruised in and out of all the creeks and bays, making maps of everything, and after an adventurous time they got safely back to Sydney. But they were not long content to remain there. Soon they started out again, and again had many adventures.

Once they got into such a storm that their little boat was nearly swamped. They themselves were soaked to the skin, their drinking water was all spoiled, and, worst of all, their gunpowder was wet and useless.

So they rowed to shore, meaning to land and dry their things, and look for fresh water. As they landed, several natives gathered round them. Bass and Flinders hardly knew what to do. The natives about were said to be very fierce, if not cannibals. There were about fifty of them, armed with spears and boomerangs, against two white men and a boy, who had no weapons, for their guns were rusty and full of sand, and their gunpowder wet.

A boomerang is a native Australian weapon made of hard wood. It is made in peculiar shape, and the black fellows throw it in such a wonderful way that it hits the object it is aimed at, and returns to the hand of the thrower.

Although very uncertain what would happen to them, Bass and Flinders put a bold face on matters. They spread out their gunpowder to dry on the rocks while the natives looked on. They next began to clean their guns, but at this the black fellows became so angry and afraid that they were obliged to stop.

As neither could understand the other's language, talking was rather difficult. But the white men made the savages understand that they wanted water, and they were shown a stream not far off where they filled their cask. They would now have been glad to get away, but their gunpowder was not dry.

Then Flinders thought of something to keep the savages interested. A few days before he had cut the hair and trimmed the beard of a savage, much to his delight. So now he produced a large pair of scissors and persuaded some of those round to let him play barber.

Flinders did not make a very good barber, but that did not matter as the savages were easily pleased. They were very proud of themselves when the cutting and snipping was done, but some of them were very much afraid as the large scissors were nourished so near their noses. Their eyes stared in wild fear, yet all the time they tried to smile as if they liked it, and they looked so funny that Flinders was almost tempted to give a little snip to their ears just to see what would happen. But the situation was too dangerous for such tricks.

At last the powder was dry. Everything was gathered and put into the boat, and the three got safely away, well pleased to have escaped while the savages were still in good humour.

A few nights after this they were nearly wrecked. They had anchored for the night when a terrible storm arose. The waves dashed high over their tiny boat, there were cliffs on one hand, reefs on the other. They hauled up their anchor as quickly as they could and ran before the gale. Bass managed the sail, Flinders steered with an oar, and the boy bailed. "A single wrong movement, a moment's inattention, would have sent us to the bottom," says Flinders.

It was an anxious time, and the darkness of the night added to their danger. But suddenly, when things were so bad that they thought they had not ten minutes more to live, the boat got through the breakers, and in three minutes the adventurers found themselves in the calm waters of a little cove. In thankfulness for their escape they called it Providential Cove. A few days later, having explored thirty or forty miles of coast, they reached Sydney in safety.

It was not long before Bass set out exploring again. This time Flinders could not go, as he had to attend to his duties on board ship. Alone Bass discovered more of the coast, but the greatest thing that he did was to make sure that Tasmania was not joined to Australia, but was a separate island. And the strait between Tasmania and Australia is called Bass Strait after him.

It would take too long to tell of all that Bass and Flinders did, and of all the adventures they had. After a little, Bass sailed away to South America on a trading expedition, and was never heard of more. It is thought that he was captured by the Spaniards, and made to work as a slave in the silver mines. If that is so, it was a terrible end for this brave sailor who loved the free life upon the ocean waves. It is pitiful to think that he, who had felt the sting of the salt spray upon his cheek, and the taste of it upon his lips, had henceforth to toil in a dark, close mine, a broken-hearted captive.

Even after his friend had gone, Flinders did a great deal of exploring. He sailed all round the coasts of Australia in a rotten, little boat called the *Investigator*. "A more deplorable, crazy vessel than the *Investigator* is perhaps not to be seen," said the captain who later, with great difficulty, brought her home to England. When Flinders reached Sydney he found that some of the planking was so soft that a stick could be poked through it. It was in such ships that those brave sailors dared the stormy seas! But Flinders was anxious to reach home, for he had made many maps of the coast, and had filled many note-books, and he wanted to have them published. So he left the *Investigator*, and sailed home as a passenger in another ship.

They had not gone far, however, when one dark and stormy night they were wrecked upon a coral reef. All night the storm raged, the winds blew, and the waves dashed over the wretched, weary men. But when morning came they saw a sandbank near, and upon this they managed to land, only three men being lost in the storm.

Luckily they were able to save most of the food and water out of the wrecked vessel, and were soon settled on their sandbank. They made tents of sails and spars, planted a flagstaff, and ran up a blue ensign with the Union Jack upside down as a signal of distress. And so they prepared to wait until some passing ship should find them and take them off. But it was by no means a likely place for ships to pass, and after a few days Flinders decided to take one of the ship's boats which had been saved from the wreck, and sail back to Sydney to bring help.

They named the little boat the *Hope*, and one fine morning Flinders, with thirteen other men, set sail. As they launched out they were followed by the cheers and good wishes of their shipwrecked comrades, and one of them, having asked leave of the captain, ran to the flagstaff, tore down the flag, and ran it up again with the Union Jack uppermost. This he did to show how sure they were that the voyage would be a success, and that Flinders would bring help.

So it was with cheerful hearts that Flinders and his brave followers began their long journey of two hundred and fifty leagues in an open boat. And like heroes they bore every hardship which came upon them. The weather became rainy and cold, and they were often drenched to the skin and had no means of drying or warming themselves. Tossed about on the huge, hollow waves like a cockle shell, in danger from sharks and whales, they yet escaped every peril, and after ten days of hardship and toil they arrived safely at Sydney.

Flinders at once went to Government House. Captain King

was by this time governor, and he was a good friend to Flinders, who now found him sitting at dinner. The governor stared in astonishment at the wild, unshorn, ragged man with lean, brown face and bright eyes, who walked into the room. It was some minutes before he knew him to be his friend Matthew Flinders, who he thought was many hundreds of miles on his way to England. But when he realised who it was, and listened to the tale of disaster, his eyes filled with tears.

At once the governor agreed to send help to the ship-wrecked men, but it was some days before ships could be got ready, and every day seemed to Flinders a week. He was so afraid that if he did not get back quickly the men on the sandbank would grow tired of waiting, give up hope, and try to save themselves in an open boat, and so perhaps all be drowned before help came.

But at length everything was ready. Three ships set sail and safely reached the narrow, sea-swept sandbank, and all the shipwrecked men were rescued.

Flinders then went on his way to England with his precious maps and plans, a few only of which had been lost in the wreck. But the ship in which he went was so small and so leaky that it could not carry enough food and water for so long a voyage. Flinders was therefore obliged to stop at every port he came to for fresh supplies. The French and British were again at war, and at Mauritius, which then belonged to France, he was taken prisoner, in spite of the fact that he had a passport from Napoleon.

Flinders was treated as a spy, and all his journals and maps were taken from him. And now his fate was little better than that of his friend Bass. For seven long years he was kept a prisoner, eating his heart out with desire for freedom. At last he was set free, and after some more adventures he reached home.

But his troubles were not at an end. He now discovered that a French sailor had stolen his maps and journal, and that he had published them in France as his own, having changed all the names which Flinders had given the places into French names. The name Australis, which Flinders had been among the first to use, he had changed to Terre de Napoleon—that is, land of Napoleon. And for many a long day Australia was marked in French atlases as Terre de Napoleon.

It was a bitter blow. But broken in health and worn with long hardships and imprisonments though he was, Flinders was not yet beaten. He gave up the rest of his life to writing an account of his travels, which he called A Voyage to Terra Australis. But, sad to say, upon the very day that it was published, he died. To the end he was a sailor and adventurer. Almost his last words were, "I know that in future days of exploration my spirit will rise from the dead and follow the exploring ships."

It was by such men of daring, by such deeds of valour and of long endurance, that the outlines of Australia were traced upon our maps.

CHAPTER IV

A LITTLE REVOLUTION

IT was in 1800 that Captain John Hunter was recalled and Captain King took his place. The new governor set himself at once to stop the trade in rum, which was bringing ruin on the Colony. Men sold everything to get it. They bartered away their sheep and cattle and even their growing corn, until they who had been prosperous farmers became ruined beggars. But in putting down the trade in rum King brought upon himself the hatred of the soldiers who made a great deal of money out of it, and who were very angry to see their gains thus disappear. He had to crush rebellions among the convicts too. The work was not easy, but King was firm, and soon he brought some kind of order out of wild confusion. And although, as he said, he " could not make pickpockets into good farmers," he forced them to be less drunken and made them try to work, and so by good behaviour earn freedom.

It was during the time of Governor King's rule that the island of Tasmania was first colonised. For sixteen years, in all the wide island-continent, it was only in the few miles round Sydney that the white man had planted his foot and built his home. But French ships were now seen cruising about, and the British began to fear that the French meant to found a colony in

Tasmania, which, since the discoveries of Bass, they knew was not joined to Australia, but was a separate island.

So to be beforehand with the French, King sent a lieutenant with a few soldiers, convicts, and freemen, to found a colony there. They landed and began to build a little town, which they called Hobart Town, in honour of Lord Hobart, who was then Secretary of State for the Colonies.

The new colony had its troubles and trials just as Sydney had had, but it conquered them all and began to prosper.

About this time, too, an attempt was made to found a town near where Melbourne now stands. But these first colonists did not think it a good place for a town. So they left their half-built houses there and went across to Tasmania, and settled down about fifteen miles from Hobart. Thus a beginning was made, and by degrees other towns were founded, and the lonely spaces of Australia began to be peopled by white men.

In 1806 Captain Bligh succeeded Captain King as governor. He was a stern, hard man with a fearful temper. He was known as "Bounty Bligh," because when he had been captain of the *Bounty* his men had mutinied and cast him adrift, with eighteen others, in an open boat in the Pacific Ocean. But however stern and cruel Bligh might be, he was a clever seaman. Now, in this terrible plight, he showed it. With wonderful skill he steered his boat and ruled his men, and after a voyage of almost four thousand miles they readied land safely. This journey of his is one of the wonderful things of the story of the sea.

But although Bligh was a good seaman he was not a good governor. He soon made himself hated by nearly every one in the colony. He quarrelled, too, with Mr. MacArthur who, you remember, had brought wool-bearing sheep to the colony and who was now, after the governor, perhaps the chief man in all Australia.

Soon after Bligh arrived MacArthur went to him to talk

about his farm and his hopes that sheep and wool would bring wealth to the colony. But Bligh flew into a temper at once. "What have I to do with your sheep and cattle?" he cried. "You have such flocks and herds as no man ever had before. You have ten thousand acres of the best land in the country. But, by heaven, you shall not keep it!"

Instead of help and sympathy, MacArthur only got angry words. So a quarrel was begun which as the months went on grew worse and worse. The fault was not all on one side, and these two strong and powerful men did not try to understand each other. At last Bligh put MacArthur into prison for refusing to pay a fine which he considered unjust. He threatened to put six officers of the " Rum Corps" in prison too, as they encouraged MacArthur.

At this, the barracks was in an uproar. Both men and officers declared that the governor was trampling on their liberty and rights, and that instead of keeping law and order he was upsetting both. They resolved not to suffer it and they rebelled.

So about half-past six one midsummer evening, which in Australia, you must remember, is in January, they gathered at the barracks. Then with fixed bayonets, drums beating, and colours flying, they marched to Government House, followed by a crowd of people all eager to see the downfall of the governor.

At the gate the governor's daughter tried to stop the soldiers. But she was told to stand aside, and the men marched unhindered into the house, for the very sentries had joined the rebels.

"I am called upon to do a most painful duty," said Major Johnston. "You are charged by the respectable inhabitants of crimes that make you unfit to rule another moment in the colony. I hereby place you under arrest by the advice of all my officers, and by the advice of every respectable inhabitant of Sydney."

Thus Bligh was taken prisoner and his rule was at an end. No one was sorry, for he had no friends. For some weeks he was kept prisoner, then promising that he would go direct to England, he was allowed to go on board a waiting vessel. But he broke his word and went to Tasmania instead. There he tried to make the colonists receive him back as governor. But although at first they treated him with all due honour, they soon grew tired of him. Bligh was then forced to leave Tasmania as he had left Australia, and for some time he cruised about in his ship.

Meanwhile Major Johnston ruled New South Wales. But after a time the news of the revolt reached England. A new governor, Colonel Macquarie, was at once sent out with a Highland regiment to restore order. Macquarie was told to make Captain Bligh governor again for twenty-four hours, just to show the mutineers that they could not do as they liked. Then he was to become governor himself and send home the whole of the New South Wales Corps, and every one who had had a part in the revolt, to answer for their misdeeds.

This was done; and the Rum Corps, which for years had been the greatest power and at times the greatest terror in the colony, went home for good and all. But no very heavy punishment was given to the mutineers. Major Johnston was expelled from the army, but he returned to Australia and became one of its most important settlers. MacArthur was forbidden to return for eight years, as he had been the chief cause of all the disturbance. But at the end of that time he did return, and his name is remembered as one of those who did most for Australia in the early days.

As for Bligh, he was made an admiral; and that, he no doubt felt, made up for all that he had gone through.

CHAPTER V

THE FIRST TRAVELLER IN QUEENSLAND

ONE day in February 1846 a ship sailed out from Sydney on its way to China. It was a cargo boat, but, as was common in those days, it carried a few passengers too, and with the captain went his wife. A fair wind blew, and all hoped for a quick and pleasant passage.

But as the ship sailed on its way the wind became ever stronger and fiercer, until, when a week from home, a terrible storm was brewing, and the ship with bare masts was scudding before the blast.

At last the storm calmed and the danger seemed over. But the ship had been driven far out of its course, and a careful watch was kept lest it should run upon some unknown rock or reef.

For a few days all went well, then suddenly one night the watchman saw something loom ahead of the ship, whether land or dark cloud he could not tell. Before anything could be done there was a fearful shock, the ship shivered from stem to stem, and then lay still.

Every one except the watchmen was in bed. The shock made them spring from their beds and rush in terror to the deck. All was black darkness. There was nothing to be seen around but the night and the cruel white-crested waves. In the darkness nothing could be done, and so in shivering misery, the waves lashing over the ship, men waited for the dawn.

The night seemed long, but at last a cold, grey light crept into the sky. Then it was seen that all around the ship sharp points of rock showed above the water. Upon one of these the ship had struck. But nowhere was there the faintest sign of land.

As soon as it was light enough, the captain ordered the boats to be lowered. But almost as soon as they reached the water, they were dashed to pieces and swept away by the savage waves.

All hope was gone, and the shipwrecked people gave themselves up to despair. But the captain was a man who did not easily give way. He ordered all hands into the cabin, and when they were gathered he bade them pray. And so there knelt together, three pale-faced women and their frightened children, with a handful of brave, rough men who well knew that they had sailed their last voyage upon this earth.

But the captain's calm voice and earnest prayer put new courage into the men. They rose from their knees and set to work to make a raft strong enough to live in that wild sea. Long they toiled, cutting and sawing, hammering and lashing spars and planks together. All the time they worked at the risk of their lives, for every wave swept the decks.

At last the raft was ready, and with great difficulty launched. What food there was, was placed upon it. But, alas, it was very little, for most of the provisions had been washed overboard or spoiled by the salt water. One cask of water, a little brandy, and nine tins of preserved meat, these were all that could be found. And with this little store the poor wrecked men set sail upon the cruel waste of waters.

Including women and children, there were twenty-one people upon the raft. They knew their food would not last long. They had all heard terrible tales of shipwrecked people, who, when they were starving, had become cannibal and had eaten each other. So now, face to face with death, they each promised solemnly to keep from anything so horrible, whatever tortures they might suffer.

At first things were just endurable. Three tablespoonfuls of meat a day were served out to each person, and four little drinks of water carefully measured. To help to eke out their stores they caught the sea-birds which now and again alighted upon the raft. These they had to eat raw, but they were looked upon as great dainties.

Three weeks passed. Both food and water were nearly done, when a sail came in sight. Eagerly the weak, worn crew waved and signed. The ship was too far away and the sailors did not see them. Hour after hour they watched and beckoned, but the sail grew smaller and smaller, and at last it vanished altogether in the dim distance, and the little raft was left once more alone on the empty sea.

The portion of meat, the measure of water, grew less and less day by day, until at last one morning there was no more meat, and no more water left. Still there was no sign of land, still there was nothing all around but the cruel, vacant sea.

"I shall die now," said one man wearily. And die he did.

Remembering their promise the others quickly threw the body overboard. They feared that the terrible pangs of hunger which had come upon them might make them forget.

But now, when there seemed nothing but an awful death before them, the poor castaways caught a fish for the first time. Each day after this they caught some fish. Then rain came and eased their terrible, burning thirst. But day by day, unable to endure longer, some of the company died. The children, two of the women, and many of the men each followed one after another.

At length, after six weeks of fearful suffering, land came in sight. Although they did not know it, the castaways had reached the shores of Queensland. They only guessed that they were somewhere on the coast of Australia.

Now when at last the raft reached the land, there were only seven left of all who had set out from the ship. These were the captain, his wife, and five men. They were little more than skeletons, and when they were once more on dry land, they lay down upon the beach and slept from sheer weakness and weariness.

Next morning the captain managed to make a fire, at which they cooked some shark which they had caught. It was the first cooked meat they had eaten for more than six weeks. Then they crawled about and found some oysters. But they were all so sick and faint with hunger and exposure, that they could with difficulty drag themselves about even in search of food.

Now again a sail was seen. With all the strength they had left, they tried to signal to it. But their efforts were in vain. Sitting on the rocks, with despair in their hearts, they watched the ship slowly sail out of sight.

Three more of the party died, and there were only four left when, to add to the terrors of the fight with death, a party of black fellows came upon them. They proved, however, in their own way, friendly. They took, it is true, everything the shipwrecked men had left, even to their clothes, leaving them almost naked. But they brought them roots to eat, and signed to them to join in their wild dance called a corrobboree.

This, of course, the white men could not do, and as the black fellows did not seem very pleased at their refusal, one of the sailors offered to sing.

This greatly delighted the savages who sat round grimacing, while the four wretched white people stood together and sang,

> God moves in a mysterious way
> His wonders to perform;
> He plants His footsteps in the sea,
> And rides upon the storm.

Thus were the white people received into the tribe. For two years they lived with the savages in great misery. They had now enough to eat, it is true, but they had to live as savages. At the end of three years all had died except one man called Murrell. He seemed better able to bear the hardships, and for seventeen years he lived among the black fellows, talking their language and living their life, until he forgot his own tongue and even his own name.

But at last, after many weary years, ships began to come, and white men, it was told Murrell, had built a hut not far off.

When he heard this news, Murrell decided to try to escape from his fearful life. So one day he set off to find the white man's hut. Having lived so many years under the burning sun of Queensland, wearing no clothes, he was very brown and very dirty too. But now when thoughts of his old life had awakened in him, he went to a pool and washed himself as white as he could.

Round the white man's hut there was a fence, and when Murrell reached it dogs ran out barking and snapping at him. So, to keep them from biting him, he climbed upon the fence and called out as loud as he could.

Three men lived in the hut, and at the sound of Murrell's call, one of them came out. He stared at this strange being in wonder. Then, "Bill," he cried, "here's a naked, yellow man standing on the fence. He isn't a black man. Bring the gun."

"Don't shoot!" cried Murrell, in terror. "I'm a shipwrecked sailor, a British object."

He really meant to say "subject," but it was so long since he had spoken English, and he was so frightened and excited, that he hardly knew what he was saying.

When the men heard him speak English they put down their gun, and brought him into the hut, listening in astonishment to his story. They gave him some breakfast, but Murrell found that he no longer liked tea; and bread, which he had not eaten for seventeen years, now seemed to choke him.

Murrell was, however, very glad to get back to civilisation once more, but he returned to his black friends to say good-bye to them. And when they understood that he was going to leave them for always they were filled with grief and cried bitterly. Murrell, too, when he thought of all the rough kindness they had shown to him these many years, was sorry to say goodbye. But the sight of white men, and the sound of his own language, had awakened all his old longing for home, and he left his black friends.

He was taken to Brisbane and made much of. He became a storekeeper, married, and settled down to a quiet life, but the terrible hardships he had passed through had left him weak and feeble, and he did not live long to enjoy his new found comforts.

Such were the adventures of the first travellers in Queensland. But things have changed. Were a traveller to land now where Murrell was shipwrecked, he would find pleasant homes and smiling pastures. And perhaps on the very spot where, seventy years ago, only the black man hunted, where Murrell wandered naked and miserable, he might find a train waiting to take him back to Brisbane.

CHAPTER VI

THROUGH THE GREAT UNKNOWN

UP to the time when Macquarie came to govern New South Wales nothing at all was known of Australia inland. The Blue Mountains, beautiful and rugged, defied every attempt to cross them. Among others, gallant George Bass had tried. But he was less successful by land than by sea and he discovered nothing.

But now the colony was growing larger, and the settlers began to feel themselves cramped between the mountains and the sea. They had need of larger pastures to feed their sheep and grow their corn, so three young men determined to find out what lay behind the mountains. And, taking with them food enough to last six weeks, they set out.

They had a hard task before them. They had to cut their way through woods where no white man at least had ever passed before. Across dark valleys, up and down steep cliffs, now crawling along narrow ledges, now clambering up rocky heights, they reached at last the western side of the hills. There they saw the land open out in rolling, fertile plains, and knew that they had found what meant new life and wealth to the colony.

"The dauntless three! for twenty days and nights
These heroes battled with the haughty heights;
For twenty spaces of the star and sun
These Romans kept their harness buckled on;

By gaping gorges, and by cliffs austere,
These fathers struggled in the great old year;
Their feet they set on strange hills scarred by fire;
Their strong arms forced a path through brake and briar;
They fought with nature till they reached the throne
Where morning glittered on the great UNKNOWN.
There, in the time of praise and prayer supreme,
Paused Blaxland, Lawson, Wentworth, in a dream;
There, where the silver arrows of the day
Smote upon slope and spire, they halted on their way.
Behind them were the conquered hills—they faced
The vast green West, with glad, strange beauty graced;
And every tone of every cave and tree
Was as a voice of splendid prophecy."

Returning home, the three told the governor of their discovery, and he, after making sure that what they said was true, set convicts to work to make a broad road across the hills. It took two years to make. Many a valley had to be bridged over, the solid rock had to be blown up. But at last the great work was finished. Then the colonists led their flocks and herds along the road to the grassy plains beyond, which were soon dotted with homesteads, and the town of Bathurst was founded.

After this many travellers set out, eager to fill the great blank of the map of Australia, and it would take many books to tell of all their adventures. With patient courage and wonderful endurance they found, and marked, and named tract after tract of the vast island, each man stealing his little corner from the Unknown and adding it to the Known. To the great work these pioneers gave their health and money and all that they had. Some of them even gave their lives, and lie lost for ever in the great, silent land, no man knowing to this day where their bones rest. Australia has no battlefields. Its peaceful soil has never been soaked in the blood of thousands, its blue skies have never been darkened with the smoke of war. No heroes have fallen to the sound of trumpet and of drum fighting for King and Country. But the men who fought with nature, who suffered hunger and thirst, and all the woes of the desert, who day by day, and hour by hour, showed the courage of endurance, are as well worth remembering as those who, in one quick moment of fervour, thought life well lost for the sake of some great cause. And the names of Hamilton, Hume, Sturt, Eyre, Leichardt, Mitchell, Kennedy and many others stand out in the story of Australia as men who were not afraid to suffer and to die.

We cannot follow all these explorers, you must read their stories elsewhere. But I will tell the story of two, not because they were the greatest or did most, but because they are among the best known, and because they were the first to cross the island-continent from south to north all the way from sea to sea. For when the island had once been crossed from shore to shore there was an end to the wonderful stories that had grown up about the marvels to be found in the middle of it. Some said that there was to be found a great and fertile land, where white people lived in the wealth and luxury of a sort of fairyland; some again said there were great inland seas, boiling rivers, and mountains of fire to be found there. But when the land had been crossed, these stories were at an end, although there was then, and is still, much to be learned.

By the year 1860 the fringes of Australia had been peopled, and although little was known of the interior, the land was divided into five colonies, broken off from the mother colony of New South Wales. Each of these colonies had a capital and a governor of its own. Victoria had its capital, Melbourne; South

Australia its capital, Adelaide; Western Australia its capital, Perth; Queensland its capital, Brisbane.

Now the Colony of Victoria decided to send out an expedition to cross the continent As its leader, an Irishman named O'Hara Burke was chosen. No expense was spared to make the expedition a success. Camels were brought on purpose from India, for they, as is well known, can go for a longer time without water than perhaps any other beast of burden. And one of the worst dangers and difficulties in Australian exploration was the want of water. It is to-day the greatest drawback to Australia.

The expedition set off from Melbourne in high spirits. Crowds of people turned out to see it start. The mayor made a speech, Burke made another, and amid a storm of good wishes and cheering the long procession of men, laden camels, and horses wound out of sight.

But the expedition which had begun so brightly was soon overshadowed. The leader of the camels quarrelled with Burke, and went back to Melbourne saying that no good would ever come of the expedition under such a leader. And indeed, brave though he was, Burke was not a good commander.

A man named Wills was now made second in command, and the expedition continued its way.

When Menindie on the Darling river was reached, it was found that some of the men and camels were already knocked up and unable to travel fast. But instead of waiting here to rest for a short time, or going on slowly, Burke, who was hot-headed and eager, divided his party into two. Leaving one half under a man named Wright to come on slowly, he pushed on quickly with Wills and six other men to Cooper's Creek. It is not easy to see what Burke hoped to gain by this, for at Cooper's Creek he arranged to wait for the others.

Here there was plenty of grass and water, and while waiting for Wright and his party to arrive, Burke and Wills made many short expeditions, exploring the country round. They found stony deserts and waterless tracts, and nothing very encouraging.

In this way a month went past. Then Burke, impatient at the slowness of Wright, decided to again divide his party. Leaving four men under a leader named Brahe to await Wright, he, with Wills and two others, again set out northward. The men left behind were told to wait three months, and if Burke and Wills did not return they might then give them up as lost and go home.

Having made all their arrangements, the little party set out. On and on, day after day, they trudged. Sometimes they met with bands of natives who, however, were friendly enough. Sometimes the way lay through stony desert, sometimes through fertile plains, or swamps and thick forest. At last they reached the seashore. But a forest of trees and a thick undergrowth of bushes lay between them and the sea, and although Burke and Wills made gallant efforts to struggle through it, they were obliged to turn back without having really seen the water or having stood upon the northern shore.

It was now two months since they had left Cooper's Creek. They were weary and worn. Their food was nearly at an end. And so they made haste to return, lest the men left at Cooper's Creek should, as they had been told, go home believing their leader to be lost in the wilds.

The way northward had seemed hard and long, the way back seemed yet harder. Soon there was nothing left to eat. One camel after another had to be killed for food. The men fell ill, and worn out with hardships, one died.

The three remaining gaunt, lean skeletons struggled on. At last they, with two skinny camels, arrived at Cooper's Creek.

There was no one there.

Upon a tree was a note telling the wretched, weary travellers that the others had left that very morning, and that Wright, who had been left behind at the Darling, had never arrived at all.

It was heart-breaking. Sick and hopeless were the men who that night lay down to sleep in the deserted camp. Burke had mismanaged the expedition badly. Perhaps he knew it, and that made the hardships no easier to bear.

Fortunately Brahe and his party had left some food behind them. They had marked a tree with the word "Dig," and here the travellers found the buried stores.

Now that they had food enough, Wills and the other man, who was called King, proposed that they should rest for a few days until they had regained some strength. But Burke with his impatient spirit would not listen. He proposed to start off again and try to reach home by going through South Australia instead of back as they had come. He wanted to go by way of Mount Hopeless, which had been reached by another explorer some years before.

There was now a sheep farm there, and Burke thought it could not be more than one hundred and fifty miles off.

It seems to us, reading of it long after, a mad and foolish idea. And so it seemed to Wills and King. But they gave way to their leader and the journey began. It was a dismal failure. They lost their way and, at last worn out and once more starving, were obliged to go back. On this return journey Burke and King became so weak that they could go no farther, and alone, Wills returned to Cooper's Creek to bring food to his dying comrades.

Meanwhile, had they only known it, help had been very near. For Brahe, having at last met with Wright, had returned to Cooper's Creek. But finding no one there, and believing that no one had been there in their absence, they all started homeward with the news that the others had perished.

The news was true enough. But it need not have been true if only things had been better managed.

Now, of the three left alone in the wilderness. Wills was the first to die. A few days later Burke followed him, and King alone was left. He kept himself from utterly starving by eating the seeds of a plant called Nardoo. Then he fell in with some friendly blacks who had already helped the forlorn party. With them he stayed until he was found and rescued, for he was not left to die unaided. When Wright and Brahe reached home with their sad news, search parties were at once sent out to find the bodies at least of the brave, misguided men. So King was found. But he was pale and thin, more like a skeleton than a living man, and so weak that he could scarcely speak. But after a few days of care and nursing he grew much better, and was able to tell the sorry story of all his pains and hardships.

The dead bodies of Burke and Wills were found where they had died, and were buried in the wilds. But afterwards they were brought to Melbourne, where they were buried with great ceremony and a monument in their memory was raised.

King received a pension, and the relatives of Burke and Wills were cared for. It is pleasant, too, to know that the kindly blacks were rewarded, although it was only with beads and ribbons, looking-glasses and sugar. To them such things seemed very precious, and they were well pleased.

"Set your face toward the darkness—tell of deserts weird and wide,
Where unshaken woods are huddled, and low languid waters glide;
Turn and tell of deserts lonely, lying pathless deep and vast;
Where in utter silence ever Time seems slowly breathing past—
Silence only broken when the sun is necked with cloudy bars,
Or when tropic squalls come hurtling underneath the sultry stars!
Deserts, thorny, hot and thirsty, where the feet of man are strange,
And eternal Nature sleeps in solitudes which know no change.

Weakened with their lengthened labours, past long plains of stone and sand,
Down those trackless wilds they wandered, travellers from a far-off land,
Seeking now to join their brothers, struggling on with faltering feet,
For a glorious work was finished, and a noble task complete;

And they dreamt of welcome faces—dreamt that soon unto their ears
Friendly greeting would be thronging, with a nation's well-earned cheers;
Since their courage never failed them, but with high, unflinching soul
Each was pressing forward, hoping, trusting all should reach the goal.

Ye must rise and sing their praises, O ye bards with souls of fire,
For the people's voice shall echo through the wailings of your lyre;
And we'll welcome back their comrade,though our eyes with tears be blind
At the thoughts of promise perished, and the shadow left behind;
Now the leaves are bleaching round them—now the gales above them glide,
But the end was all accomplished, and their fame was far and wide.
Though this fadeless glory cannot hide a nation's grief,
And their laurels have been blended with a gloomy cypress wreath.

Let them rest where they have laboured! but, my country, mourn and moan;
We must build with human sorrow grander monuments than stone,
Let them rest, for oh! remember, that in long hereafter time
Sons of Science oft shall wander o'er that solitary clime!
Cities bright shall rise about it. Age and Beauty there shall stray,
And the fathers of the people, pointing to the graves, shall say:
Here they fell, the glorious martyrs! when these plains were woodland deep;
Here a friend, a brother, laid them; here the wild man came to weep."

                                              H. C. KENDALL

CHAPTER VII

"THE TRACTS OF THIRST AND FURNACE"

A S years went on and Australia grew, great farms stretched out from the towns into the wilds. Many a farmer owned a sheep- or cattle-run as big as an English county, and the yellowing cornfields reached for miles waving and beautiful in the sunshine.

The soil of Australia is in many places so fertile and the climate so good that farming is easy. But the farmers have one great trouble. That is the want of a good water supply. In Australia there are no high mountains to catch the rain clouds. There are no big inland lakes or rivers, and a curious thing about the Australian rivers is that many of them instead of flowing to the sea flow inland. When a drought comes, some of these rivers disappear altogether, and sometimes a drought will last for months or even years.

The years 1839-1840 were years of terrible drought. The grass became browner and browner, and at last it was burnt up altogether and only the dry, sandy earth remained. The leaves withered on the trees and shrivelled up. There was no coolness anywhere. The wind was hot like the blast of a furnace, and, as it swept through the forests, the leaves hissed and crackled against each other instead of whispering gently with a cool, soft sound. No green thing was to be seen, the still air quivered with heat, and the silent birds fell dead from the branches.

The cattle, daily growing thinner and thinner, wandered farther and farther over the plains in search of food and water. As the water pools dried up, the weaker animals sank into the mud and sand left on the edge, and having no strength to struggle out again died there. And there they lay, their dead bodies poisoning the air until the plain was strewn with bleaching bones.

Corn, too, ceased to grow, and flour was sold at £100 a ton. Starvation and ruin stared many a farmer in the face. At first they tried to drive their cattle to Sydney to sell them to the butchers there. But as every one wanted to sell, there were not enough people to buy, and the cattle before they reached Sydney were often little more than skin and bone.

It was then that a Mr. O'Brien thought of a plan by which something might be saved. He had heard that in Russia, when farmers had too many cattle, they killed them for their fat, for though the butchers in a town could only buy a certain amount of meat, a market for tallow could always be found, for it could be sent to distant lands. So now factories and places for boiling down sheep and cattle were built both in Sydney and in the country, and to the farmers' great delight they found that they could make a little out of their starving cattle. Valuable cattle were killed merely for their skin and tallow, but it was better to make even a few pounds than nothing at all, and the poor beasts were put out of misery. The meat of course was wasted, but some of it was used as manure for the land. And sometimes a butcher would buy a hundred or two legs of mutton at 1d. each, and make a good profit out of them by selling them to his customers for so much a pound. Thus many of the colonists were saved from utter ruin, and able to live until the rain came again.

When at last the rain did come in a few weeks, the earth was, as if by magic, covered with green once more. Then the cattle, which had wandered in helpless pain, dull-eyed, pitiful skeletons, again became sleek and lively. But in places the rain came with such sudden fury that the river-beds could not contain it, and great floods were the consequence. Then perhaps what a farmer had saved from the drought would be torn from him by the flood.

About ten years later another drought withered the land. Rivers and water-pools disappeared, the earth became a sun-baked desert of clay, where great cracks yawned, and where the cattle wandered "with the terror of thirst in their eyes." As the summer went on, the air grew hotter and hotter, the sky a brazen bowl. Then in February came a day which in Victoria is remembered as Black Thursday. From the north a hot wind blew with the breath of a furnace. The sky grew dark, and out in the Bass Straits weather-wise sailors furled their sails, and made ready to meet a fearful storm.

Hour by hour the wind gathered strength and speed, till by midday it tore shrieking through the bare, scorched trees, howling over the plains, where the bones of hundreds of cattle lay bleaching. Then to the howl and shriek of the wind was added the roar and crackle of fire. As if by magic the whole land was sheeted in flame. On it came like some hungry demon, fierce tongues of fire licking the earth, pillars of smoke climbing the sky. The raging wind tore the lifeless leaves from the trees, the arid grass from the plain, and in a whirl of sparks swept them on to kindle into fresh flame wherever they fell.

The fiery monster spared nothing. The great forest trees appeared for a few minutes pillared and arched in flame, then sank together in one huge bonfire. Farmhouses and gardens were swept away, and as the flames rolled on, man and beast fled before them vainly seeking shelter. Wherever water was to be found, there men fled. Standing in the water they waited, blinded and gasping in the smoke-laden air, till the column of fire had rolled past Above the roar of the flames rose the scream and bellow of terrified animals, the thud and patter of a thousand hoofs, as horse and bullock, sheep and kangaroo, all the beasts of field or forest, birds and serpents, and every living thing, fled before the fiery sword of destruction. Driven by a nameless terror, panting to escape from an awful death, they fled.

All day long and far into the night the storm of fire lasted, and when morning dawned, the land in its track lay a black ruin of desolation.

Many men, women, and children, had died in the flames. Many more lost all that they possessed, and, penniless and disheartened, had to begin life over again, had again to build their homesteads and fence their runs, and find money to buy new tools and a fresh stock of cattle. It was never known how much was lost in this great fire, but those who lived in the country at the time never forgot the havoc it made, or the terrible devastation it left behind. But at length rain came again. Then in a far shorter time than we should believe possible, the land that had been a charred and smoking desert was once more green pasture and corn land, dotted with pleasant homesteads, and Black Thursday was no more than a memory.

CHAPTER VIII

THE FINDING OF GOLD

NEAR the town of Bathurst there lived a farmer called Hargraves. He had suffered much from the droughts, and at last, tired of the struggle, he gave up his farm and sailed away to California. He went to try his luck at the goldfields which had lately been discovered there. But in California Hargraves was no more lucky than he had been in New South Wales. Although others around him made fortunes, he made none. However, as he dug, and shovelled, and toiled in vain, a strange thought struck him. The hills and valleys of California were very like the hills and valleys of New South Wales, he said to himself. If there was gold to be found in the one, why not in the other?

When this idea had once taken hold of Hargraves he could not get rid of it. So at length he made up his mind to leave his useless toil and go back to Australia to find out if there was anything in his idea.

He had now very little money left, but he managed to get back to Sydney. He arrived there penniless, and had to borrow money in order to hire a horse to take him to the Blue Mountains, for in those days there were no trains.

At a lonely inn on the slopes of the mountains he put up his horse. There he found a boy who knew all the creeks and streams about, and, with him as guide, Hargraves started out early one morning carrying a trowel and a little tin dish.

Soon he came to what he thought was a likely place in which to find gold. Digging up a little of the greyish, sandy soil he went with it to the nearest stream. Here he dipped and dipped his tin in the water until all the sand was washed away. Then, there at the bottom, too heavy to be floated away by the water, lay a few small grains of dull, glowing gold.

As time after time Hargraves filled his little tin pan, and saw the tiny grains of precious metal glow at the bottom, his breath came fast, his eyes sparkled, his cheeks glowed with triumph. He knew that he had found what he sought, and that fortunes for thousands lay hidden in the hills around him.

Tired, but rejoicing, he went back to his inn and wrote down all that he had done, very sure that he had found out something great, not only for himself, but for all Australia.

For two months Hargraves remained among the lonely hills making quite certain of his discovery. Then he went back to Sydney and wrote a letter to the governor, saying that for £500 he would show him places in New South Wales where gold could be found.

Many people had pretended to find gold before this. So now the governor was not very ready to believe Hargraves. However, he said that if Hargraves would first point out the place, he would be rewarded afterwards.

This Hargraves agreed to, and in a week there were a thousand people digging and washing for gold in that lonely creek, which, a month or two before, had echoed to the shouts of one man and a boy.

The rush to the diggings was tremendous. Farmers left their farms, doctors their patients. Labourers, servants, clerks, workmen of all kinds, thieves and cutthroats, all swelled the stream which poured along the road over the Blue Mountains.

It was hardly to be wondered at that people would no longer toil all day long for a few shillings, when, in the same time they might, by scratching the earth a little, win hundreds of pounds. So business came to a standstill, grass grew in the streets, corn stood in the fields uncut, even the ships remained idle in the harbour, for the sailors deserted whenever they could, and made for the diggings.

But although many who went to the mines made fortunes, others, like Hargraves himself in California, returned in a few weeks disappointed and angry. Others, too, went thinking that they had nothing to do but pick up lumps of gold and carry it home in cart-loads. When these found that they had to work hard, to dig, and shovel, and wash, perhaps for weeks, to live in a tent and "do" for themselves, they were disgusted, and they, too, trooped homewards. All these disappointed people thought that Hargraves had fooled them, and could they have found him they would have gladly killed him. But he kept out of the way.

So over the road between Sydney and the diggings there was a constant double stream of people, some going, eager to begin work, others returning, grumbling and discontented.

But although some returned disappointed, the rush to the goldfields continued so great that it seemed as if all the other colonies would be emptied of men, and that their whole life would come to a standstill. So to stop the rush of settlers out of Victoria, the government there offered a reward to any one who would find gold in Victoria. Gold was found, and found in far richer quantities than in New South Wales. The rush was then turned in another direction, but it still went on. Indeed Melbourne was left at one time with only one policeman on duty. But that did not matter much, as all the rascals and thieves had gone to the diggings like other people. Some marched along with a pack on their back holding all that they possessed in the world, picnicking on the way, sleeping in the open air. Others,

"ALL DAY LONG THE SOUND OF THE PICK AND THE RUMBLE OF THE CRADLE WERE HEARD."

a little better off, had hand-barrows in which to carry their goods, while those still better off rode along on horseback or in light gigs or buggies. But all hurried in one direction, all had one object—gold.

At first it was only the colonists who swarmed to the gold-fields, for it was some months before the news reached home. In those days there was no telegraph to Australia, and boats took three months to cross the seas. But when at last the news did reach home, whole shiploads of men from almost every nation in Europe came thronging to the diggings. There were among them old and young, rich and poor, strong and feeble, and even the lame and the blind.

To find the gold there was little skill needed and few tools. A pick, a shovel, a pan, and a cradle were enough. The cradle was a pan on rockers into which the earth containing the gold was put along with water, and rocked about until all the sand and earth was washed away and only the gold remained.

All over the country new towns sprang up—towns of tents and wooden shanties. There all day long, from dawn to dusk, the sound of the pick and the rumble of the cradle was heard. Then at the sound of a gun all work ceased. The diggers scattered to their tents, fires were lit, and supper was cooked. For a little there was no noise except the clatter of billies or pans in which tea was boiled, and the hum of talk. Supper over, the men sat around the glowing fires smoking and telling tales, and singing songs, while overhead the stars came out and quiet darkness settled all about them. Then after a time the sounds of song and laughter would cease, and silence would reign over the little town till morning.

In those early days many people made great fortunes in a few weeks, or sometimes by some lucky find, in one day. Others returned home as poor as they had set out, and broken in health. And some who made great fortunes spent it as quickly as they had made it. They did all kinds of wild things simply to get rid of their money, such as buying pianos which they could not use, and having champagne in bucketfuls.

Many lumps of gold called nuggets were found, some of them so large that one was enough to make a man's fortune. One called the Kerr nugget was found by a black shepherd near Bathurst. He had heard how white men were going almost mad seeking for gold, so while he guarded his sheep, he amused himself by poking about with a stick to see if he also could not find some of the mysterious treasure. And in this way, one day he came upon a lump so large that even he, who knew nothing of the value of it, grew excited.

Running back to the farmhouse he burst in upon his master and mistress as they were sitting down to dinner. "O massa!" he cried, hardly able to speak for excitement and breathlessness, "white man find little fellow, me find big fellow!"

When the shepherd had explained what he meant, his master put to his horse and drove off to see this wonderful nugget. There, sure enough, was a huge lump of gold sticking out of the ground where every one might see it, and only needing to be picked up. It was truly a "big fellow," and so heavy that it had to be broken in two before it could be carried away. It afterwards sold for £4000.

But although the Kerr was one of the first large nuggets, it was by no means the largest. Others worth more than double were found later, to which people gave names such as Blanche Barkly, Welcome Nugget, and Welcome Stranger.

Soon the tented mushroom towns grew larger and more numerous. Theatres, hotels, and even churches were built. But when a mine became exhausted, or when news of a richer mine reached the diggers, the township would be deserted, and the country sink back to its former peace, only hundreds of little sand heaps being left to show where men had lately toiled like a swarm of busy ants.

Things were not always quiet and orderly on the goldfields. The greed of gain and the thirst for gold brought out man's evil passions, and often dark and dreadful deeds were done.

Every digger, too, had to pay thirty shillings a month to the government for leave to dig. To the lucky ones who were making fortunes that seemed nothing. To the unlucky ones who toiled for days finding little it seemed a great deal, and they tried to avoid paying it. Upon every goldfield there was a force of police. These police could demand to see a man's licence, and if he had none they carried him off to prison. So many of the diggers came to look upon the police as their enemies, and there were often fights between them.

But those days have long since passed. Gold digging still goes on in Australia. But it is very different now. The men no longer work with pick and shovel, they no longer make fortunes in a single day. The mines are owned by companies, the men are paid wages like any other miners, and the work is done by machinery with all the latest improvements and inventions. And the news of the opening of a new mine or the finding of a large nugget no longer drives people from their offices and their desks to seek their fortunes at the diggings.

CHAPTER IX

THE BUSHRANGERS

"Hunted, and haunted, and hounded,
Outlawed from human kin,
Bound with the self-forged fetters
Of a long career of sin,
Hands that are red with slaughter,
Feet that are sunk in crime—
A harvest of tares and thistles
For the pending scythe of Time."

JENNINGS CARMICHAEL

IN the early days of Australia one of the great terrors and dangers of a country life was the bushrangers.

"Bush" meant all land unknown and unreclaimed beyond the few towns and settlements. It might be "open bush," "thick bush," or "scrubby bush"—it was all bush, whether dark forest with high trees and tangled vines, or great plains of tall, waving grass. And the bushrangers were the brigands of the wilds—the Robin Hoods of the Australian forests, except that the bushrangers were, as a rule, brutal and bad, and we have come to think that Robin Hood was a good fellow.

Bushrangers were at first convicts who had escaped into the wilds. For as convicts were hired out to farmers and others as servants, it was much easier for them to escape than it is for a gang of prisoners working under the eye of a warder. Sometimes as many as thirty or forty would escape in a year. They fled to the woods, often living with the savages and doing dreadful deeds. They thought little of committing a murder for a meal, but many of their wicked deeds were done out of a kind of wild revenge for having been imprisoned. Now and again, however, the life in the bush would prove too hard even for these criminals, and after suffering fearful hardships they would return, begging to be forgiven and taken back.

But enough remained to become a terror to the peaceful inhabitants. And at one time, both in Tasmania and in New South Wales, the bushrangers became so bad that the settlers worked in the fields with pistols in their belts, and the women in the houses kept loaded guns always to hand.

One of the most famous Tasmanian bushrangers was Michael Howe. He was a convict who had been a sailor, and who had been condemned to seven years' hard labour for robbery. But not long after he arrived in Tasmania, Howe escaped and joined a band of bushrangers. He soon became their chief, and he ruled like a tyrant. He was very haughty, calling himself "The Governor of the Ranges." The governor of the colony he called the "Governor of the Town."

Howe and his gang soon became the terror of the neighbourhood, but although £100 was offered for his head, none dared try to earn it, for most feared him too much, while others admired him.

At last an old sailor named Worral, also a convict, determined to win the reward. Helped by two other men, he hunted his prey for many days, and at last tracked him to his hiding-place. He was a strange figure, this wild terror of the hills. Clothed in kangaroo skin, with a haversack and powder-flask across his shoulders, and a long, dark beard flowing over his breast, he faced his enemies. Howe fought well for his life, but the struggle was short, and he fell to the ground. Then hacking off his head. Worral carried it, a ghastly prize, to the governor, much as in days long, long ago men carried the heads of wolves to the king for a reward. Worral received his promised reward, and was sent home a free man, loaded now, not with fetters, but with the thanks both of colonists and governor.

Years went on, and convicts were no longer sent to Australia. For as more and more free settlers came, they began to object to the convicts being sent there. Into South Australia they had never been allowed to enter. And in 1868, just eighty years after Sydney had been first founded, the last convict-ship sailed for Australia. After that, evildoers were shut up in prisons at home.

But although convicts no longer came, bushrangers did not die out. Others took to the wild life. Sometimes they were the descendants of these convicts or of ticket-of-leave men, as freed convicts were called, or others who had a grudge against mankind, and hated law and order, and above all hated work. They were wild, fearless men, splendid horsemen, deadly shots.

In the great pastures of Australia horses and cattle are not shut into small, fenced fields as at home, but each animal has the initial of its owner branded on its hide. There were men who made a trade of stealing cattle. With a hot iron they changed the letters of the brand, and drove the beasts off to some town far enough away where buyers could be found who would not ask too many questions about where they had come from. These men were called "cattle-duffers" or "bushwhackers." They often carried on their trade for years, but when they became known, and the police were in search of them, they would take to the bush and become regular bushrangers.

Then when gold was found bushrangers became yet more rife. For the gold had to be carried to towns or to the coast to be shipped home. It went always guarded by troops or policemen,

"THE COACH WOULD BE 'HELD-UP' AND ALL THE PASSENGERS ROBBED."

but gangs of bushrangers banded together and very often managed to carry off the treasure. Or sometimes the coach, which carried miners and others from the mines to the towns, would be "held up" and all the passengers robbed.

One of the most dreaded of bushrangers was a man called Daniel Morgan. He was a wild, bad man, and, unlike other bushrangers, he was always alone. He was utterly brutal, and his one desire seemed to be to kill. One day he walked into a farmhouse, alone as usual, with a pistol in either hand and demanded brandy. It was given to him, and then, either from drunkenness or mere cruelty, he began firing among the men with his pistols. Three of them were so badly wounded that one man asked leave to go for a doctor. Morgan said he might go, but when the farmer was on his horse he repented, and, firing at him from behind, shot him dead.

With such doings as these Morgan kept the countryside a-tremble. But at last he came to his end.

The dreaded bushranger appeared one evening at a farmhouse called Peachelba, owned by a Mr. MacPherson. He ordered tea, and after tea commanded Mrs. MacPherson to play upon the piano. With trembling fingers the poor lady did her best. But, as you may imagine, at such a time she could not give her mind to piano-playing, and all the thanks she got was to be yelled at and told that she played very badly.

All the household had been gathered into the room by Morgan's orders, so that he might have them under his eye and pistol Only one little child who was ill was allowed to stay in bed. But now the child began to cry, and Mrs. MacPherson begged to be allowed to send her servant to look after it.

Morgan gruffly gave permission, and the servant left the room. Presently the crying ceased, and Mrs. MacPherson, looking out of the window, saw some one running from the house.

It was the servant. As fast as her feet could carry her she ran to another farm near. Panting and breathless, she rushed into the house and told her news. "But I must go back," she added, "or he will miss me."

"All right," said the farmer, and the brave servant fled back again and returned to the sick child before any one, except Mrs. MacPherson, knew that she had been out of the house.

Quickly the farmer sent messages to the country round about, and by morning twenty-eight men had gathered to surround Peachelba, eager to catch Morgan.

It was a long, weary night to the folk at the farm, but at last day dawned. Breakfast over, Morgan picked up his pistols. "Now, MacPherson," he said, "we will go and get a horse."

MacPherson agreed, for he could do nothing else. But as they walked to the yard a man suddenly slipped from behind a tree. He levelled a gun, there was a loud report, and the dreaded Morgan fell to the ground. Then as if by magic men hurried from their hiding-places and surrounded him. A few hours later Morgan died, having hardly spoken except to grumble that he had not been challenged to a fight—had not had a "fair chance."

A very famous band of bushrangers was a gang called the Kellys. The whole family, both men and women, were a wild, horse-stealing, house-breaking lot. So much feared were they that the country they lived in came to be known as the Kelly district. But they, too, came to their end. Ned Kelly was hanged, others of the gang met their deaths in different ways, and the country settled down into peace once more. But so famous had they been that a theatre manager bought their horses, and made a good deal of money by bringing them into a Christmas pantomime in Melbourne.

Now, happily, the bushranger has gone from the land of Australia as pirates have vanished from the seas. And we may be glad. Their doings may make thrilling stories to read, but most of us would rather not meet them in real life. And it is strange to think that they lived so lately. Robin Hood seems a long way off in the story of our little island, but it is less than thirty years since the last Australian bushranger met his death, and there are men still living who can remember the days when Morgan and the Kellys and others like them held the countryside in thrall.

But Australia is a country which makes rapid strides. One hundred and eighty years ago there was no such place, so far as the white man was concerned. Now in the Island-Continent there are more than five million white people. And what is more wonderful is that a whole continent is under one flag, a thing which in the history of the world has never been before, not even in the days of Alexander, of Cæsar, or of Napoleon. And that flag is the red, white, and blue—the Union Jack. For although since 1901, when all the five colonies united in one, Australia has been a commonwealth, it is still a part of the British Empire.

LIST OF KINGS AND GOVERNORS

KINGS OF GREAT BRITAIN AND IRELAND.		GOVERNORS OF NEW SOUTH WALES.		
George III., ...	1760			
		Captain Arthur Phillip,	1787 to 1792	
		Major Grose, . . .	1792 ,,	1795
		Captain John Hunter, .	1795 ,,	1800
		Captain King, . .	1800 ,,	1806
		Captain Bligh, . .	1806 ,,	1808
		Major-General Macquarie,	1808 ,,	1821
George IV., ...	1820			
		Sir Thomas Brisbane, .	1822 ,,	1825
		Sir Ralph Darling, .	1825 ,,	1831
William IV., . . .	1830			
		Sir Richard Bourke, .	1831 ,,	1838
Victoria, ...	1837			
		Sir George Gipps, . .	1838 ,,	1846
		Sir Charles Fitzroy, .	1846 ,,	1855
		Sir William Denison, .	1855 ,,	1861
		Sir John Young, . .	1861 ,,	1867
		(Lord Lisgar)		
		Lord Belmore, .	1868 ,,	1872
		Sir Hercules Robinson, .	1872 ,,	1879
		Lord Loftus, . .	1879 ,,	1885
		Lord Carrington, .	1885 ,,	1890
		Earl Jersey, . .	1890 ,,	1893
		Sir J. Duff, . .	1893 ,,	1894
		Viscount Hampden, .	1894 ,,	1899
		GOVERNORS-GENERAL OF THE COMMONWEALTH OF AUSTRALIA.		
		Lord Hopetoun, . .	1900 ,,	1902
Edward VII., . . .	1901			
		Lord Tennyson, .	1902 ,,	1904
		Lord Northcote, .	1904 ,,	1908
		Earl Dudley, . .	1908 ,,	1911
George V., ...	1910			
		Lord Denman, . .	1911	

NEW ZEALAND

CHAPTER I

HOW A GREAT WHITE BIRD CAME TO THE SHORES

IT is doubtful what white man first saw the shores of New Zealand. But the honour is generally given to the Dutch discoverer Tasman. In 1642, returning to Batavia, after having discovered Tasmania, he came upon South Island. Hoping to get fresh water and green food to supply his ship, he anchored. Soon canoes pushed out from the shore, and wild, half-naked savages surrounded Tasman's two ships. They called to the white strangers in loud, rough voices, and blew upon a harsh sounding trumpet. But they would not come within a stone's throw of the ships, although Tasman tried to entice them with presents of linen and knives.

Seeing the natives so many and so warlike, Tasman thought that it would be well to warn the sailors in the other ship to be on their guard, and not let them come aboard. So he ordered a boat to be lowered. But as soon as the natives saw the boat in the water, they surrounded it and drove their canoes crashing against its sides, so that it heeled over. The savages then attacked the Dutchmen with their paddles and short, thick clubs. Three were killed, and one wounded so badly that he died; the others jumped into the water and swam to their ship, while the savages made off, taking one of the dead Dutchmen with them.

Now all hope of friendly barter with the natives being at an end, Tasman sailed away. In memory of this cruel greeting from the savages, he called the place Murderer's Bay, but the name has since been changed to Golden Bay. The whole land Tasman called Staten Land, but that name, too, was soon changed to New Zealand, which name it has kept ever since. And, although we have come to think of it as an English name, it is really Dutch, for the new found land was called after that part of Holland called Zeeland.

But although Tasman had discovered and named New Zealand, no white man had yet set foot upon its shores. The Dutch made no use of their discovery, and for many years the wild Maoris, as the natives of New Zealand are called, were left undisturbed. Now and again a ship touched upon the shores, but little was known of the island until, a hundred years and more after Tasman had sailed away, when another great sailor reached them. This was Captain James Cook.

In 1769 Cook set out upon a voyage of discovery, and before he reached the Great South Land, he came upon the shores of New Zealand. He touched the shores, not on the west side as Tasman had done, but on the east coast at Poverty Bay. Here he landed, being the first white man who is known certainly to have set foot upon these islands.

To the natives the coming of Cook was a thing of fear and wonder. As the Endeavour, with outspread sails, came nearer and nearer, they watched the great, white bird, as they took it to be, in amazement, marvelling at the size and beauty of it's wings. Presently the white bird folded it's wings, and from it's side down dropped a tiny wingless bird. This, as it came near, they saw was a curious canoe, filled with white-faced gods. At the sight they turned and fled away in terror. But soon taking courage, they returned brandishing long, wooden spears, and seeming so ready to fight that Cook's men fired upon them.

"COOK TOLD THE MAORIS THAT HE HAD COME TO SET A MARK UPON THEIR ISLANDS."

And thus upon the very first day on which the white man came, blood stained the ground.

From Poverty Bay, Cook sailed northward, meeting often with savages. Sometimes they were friendly, and would barter honestly with the ship's crew. At other times they were warlike or thievish, stealing what they could, and singing loud war-songs in defiance.

Cook had with him a South Sea Islander called Tupia, who helped him very much to become friendly with the savages. For although their languages were not quite the same, they could understand each other. So Tupia was able to tell the savages that Cook came in a friendly way, and did not want to fight.

At Mercury Bay, Cook again landed, set up the Union Jack, carved the ship's name and the date upon a tree, and claimed the land for His Majesty, King George. Then sailing onward, he passed all round North Island, and through Cook's Strait (named after himself), proving thus to himself and his crew that these lands were indeed islands, and not part of a continent as had been thought.

At Queen Charlotte's Sound, upon South Island, Cook set up two posts, one on the mainland and one on a little island. Upon these posts were carved the ship's name, the month, and the year, and from the top of them the Union Jack fluttered out.

A few natives came to watch these strange doings, and Cook told them that he had come to set a mark upon their islands, in order to show any ship that might put in there that he had been before them. So the savages allowed him to put up the posts, and promised never to pull them down. They did not understand, however, that Cook, in the manner of those days, was claiming their land in the name of a king who lived in another island, far far away.

After setting up the Union Jack on Queen Charlotte Sound, Cook sailed all round South Island and Stewart Island, and upon 1st April 1770, he left the coast, and steered for the Great South Land.

Cook discovered many interesting things about New Zealand. Among other things, he found out that except a few rats and a few ugly dogs, there were no four-footed animals in the islands at all. Both rats and dogs were used for food, but the natives chiefly lived on eels, fish, and fern-root. New Zealand is the land of ferns, and every valley and hillside is green with them. With the Maoris, fern-root took the place of corn with us, for in New Zealand, although the land was fertile and good, no grain of any kind grew. Fern-root was first roasted, then beaten into a greyish kind of meal, from which bread was made.

The Maoris were tall, strong men of a brownish colour. Their hair was black, and they wore it tied into a bunch on the top of the head, into which they stuck a black, red, or white feather. The faces of the chiefs were tattooed all over in wonderful patterns, the less important people painted themselves with red ochre.

They were a savage and ignorant people, but brave and warlike. Many of them did not care in the least for beads and ribbons and things which usually pleased savages. They thought much more of iron nails, knives, and hatchets. But although they were such fine men, there was one very bad and horrible thing about them. They were cannibals.

The islands were filled with many tribes, who were constantly quarrelling and fighting with each other. Very little was enough to make a quarrel, for the Maoris were terribly proud. A blow was a deadly insult which could only be wiped out in blood, and after a battle the victors would make a horrid feast upon the bodies of their fallen foes. That a chief should be eaten was counted a great disgrace to his tribe, for it was a proof of defeat. And to say to a Maori that his father had been eaten was an insult beyond all words. To have killed and eaten many enemies was a warrior's brightest glory, and great men were often called 'eaters of chiefs.'

In seven years Cook paid five visits to New Zealand. Each time he discovered more of the coast, and learned more of the people and their customs. He brought with him pigs, fowls, potatoes, maize, and other plants and animals likely to be of use to the savages. Some of the plants and animals died, but both pigs and potatoes soon grew plentiful in the land.

CHAPTER II

THE APOSTLE OF NEW ZEALAND

AFTER Cook, the next visitors to New Zealand were Frenchmen. In those days, as soon as a new land was discovered, wonderful stories were told about it. And the Frenchmen, having heard that the British had discovered an island full of gold and precious stones, came to see, and, if possible, get some of it for themselves. They fell into quarrels and misunderstandings with the natives, and horrible massacres took place. Soon tales of the cruel, man-eating savages who lived in New Zealand spread far and wide. It was not long before the islands got such an evil name that sailors avoided the shores with horror. Men thirsting for fresh water, dying for want of fresh food, chose rather to die than to run the risk of falling into the hands of cannibal savages.

But in spite of its evil name, there were still some roving, daring Britons who ventured to the shores to barter with the savages. For New Zealand flax was so soft and silky that manufacturers were eager to buy it. New Zealand timber, too, was sought after, and above all it was found to be a splendid sealing and whaling ground. So for the sake of wealth men were found to brave the terrors of these shores.

But these old sealers and whalers were among the wildest

and most reckless of men. They treated the Maoris and their customs with contempt. They carried them off, both men and women, as slaves, and again and again the proud savages repaid such treatment with a terrible vengeance.

Vainly good men, seeing these things, appealed to King George to put a stop to them. The answer was "The islands are not within His Majesty's dominions." The Governor of New South Wales tried to protect the savages, and threatened those who ill-treated them with punishments. That, too, was vain. For in those days many white men regarded a savage as little better than a beast, to be hunted and hounded as such.

Besides being brave and warlike, the Maoris were a roving, sea-loving people like the Britons themselves. Long ages before white men had touched their shores, they, too, had come from far distant islands, and made a new home in New Zealand. The story of their wanderings had been handed down from father to son, and the names of the canoes in which they had come were still remembered among them.

Now that white men came again and again from far over the seas, the roving spirit awoke once more in many of the Maoris. They longed to see the land from which these white-faced strangers came; these strangers who carried thunder and lightning in their hands, and spoke death to their enemies from afar. They wanted, too, to see the great chief of this powerful nation, for they thought he must be indeed a mighty warrior. So some of the Maoris ventured on board the whaling vessels and sailed away to England. Some of them, too, saw King George, but when they saw that he was a feeble, old man and no warrior at all, they were greatly disappointed.

Some Maoris, too, sailed to Sydney. There they met a man whose name stands out in the early story of New Zealand almost more than any other. This man was Samuel Marsden, who has been called the "Apostle of New Zealand."

Marsden was prison chaplain at Sydney. He had done much good work among the rough, bad convicts, and when he came to know the wild, ignorant, misunderstood savages, he longed to help them too. "They are as noble a race of men as are to be met with in any part of the world," he wrote to a friend. "I trust I shall be able in some measure to put a stop to those dreadful murders which have been committed upon the islands for some years past, both by Europeans and by the natives. They are a much injured people notwithstanding all that has been said against them."

Among the Maoris whom Marsden met was a chief called Ruatara. He was one of those who had travelled to Europe. There he had had many adventures, and had been cruelly treated by the white men in whom he had trusted. He was returning home, poor and miserable, when Marsden met and befriended him. And when after more adventures he at length reached New Zealand again, he carried with him the story of Marsden's kindness, making his countrymen believe that all white men were not treacherous and base.

Ruatara also carried home with him a present of wheat which Marsden had told him how to sow.

The wheat was sown, and grew, and ripened. But the Maoris scoffed. They did not believe Ruatara's tale that flour could be made from these thin, yellow stalks. But strong in his faith in his new friend, Ruatara reaped and threshed the wheat. Then he came to a standstill. The Maori savages had no idea of the roughest or simplest kind of mill. Ruatara did not know how to grind his wheat, and laughter against him grew louder than ever. But Marsden had not forgotten his friend, and soon a ship arrived bringing the present of a hand-mill.

In great excitement Ruatara called his friends together. They gathered round him, still scoffing. But when a stream of flour flowed from the mill they were lost in wonder. As soon as enough flour was ground it was carried off, hastily made into a cake, and cooked in a frying pan. Then the Maoris danced and sang for joy. Ruatara had spoken the truth. Henceforth he was to be believed, and they were ready to receive his friend Marsden with kindness.

Soon after this Marsden got leave from his work in New South Wales and visited New Zealand. He landed in the Bay of Islands, on the north-east coast of North Island. In this very bay, not long before, the crew of a British ship had been cruelly slaughtered, and many of them devoured by the savage victors. Yet without one thought of fear Marsden landed among these man-eaters.

Marsden brought with him, as a present from the Governor of New South Wales, three horses, two cows, and a bull. None of the Maoris, except the two or three like Ruatara who had travelled, had ever seen a horse or a cow. They had never seen any animal bigger than a pig, so they wondered greatly at these large, strange beasts. And when Marsden mounted one of the horses and rode along the sands, they wondered still more.

At this time a fierce war was raging in the Bay of Islands between Ruatara and his uncle Hongi on the one side, and a tribe called the Whangaroans on the other side. Marsden was already known as the friend of Ruatara. Now he determined to make friends with the Whangaroans and bring peace between the foes.

These were the very savages who not long before had killed and eaten the British sailors. Yet Marsden made up his mind to spend a night among them. Taking only one friend with him, Marsden went first to the camp of Hongi. Hongi was a very great and fierce warrior, but Samuel Marsden had won his heart, and with him he was gentle and kind. In Hongi's camp the missionaries had supper and then walked to the enemy's camp, which was about a mile away.

The Whangaroan chiefs received the white strangers kindly. They all sat down together, the chiefs surrounding the two white men. The summer sun was setting, night was coming on, they were alone among cannibals, yet they felt no fear.

Marsden began to talk, telling the Maoris why he had come. He was the friend of Hongi and Ruatara, he said, he wished to be their friend, too, and bring peace among them. Marsden could not speak the Maori language so one chief, who like Ruatara had travelled, and could speak English, translated all that Marsden said.

Long they talked. The sun set, the sky grew dark, the stars shone out. One by one the savages lay down to rest upon the ground. At length Marsden, too, and his friend wrapped themselves in their greatcoats and lay down.

But for Marsden there was little sleep. He lay awake, watching and thinking. It was a strange scene. Above twinkled the bright stars, in front lay the sea, calm and smooth, the waves splashing softly against the shore. Far off in the bay shone the lights of the waiting ship, but close around the white men rose a forest of spears, stuck upright in the ground. All over the plain lay huddled groups of man-eating savages, sleeping peacefully. And who could be sure that they would not suddenly spring up and slay the two white men to make a morning feast?

But the night passed, and with daylight came a boat from the ship to take Marsden and his friend on board again. Marsden asked all the chiefs to come too, although he doubted if they would trust themselves in his power, knowing how often they had been deceived by wicked white men. They showed, however, no sign either of fear or anger, and went on board the ship quite willingly. First Marsden gave them breakfast, then he gathered them all into the cabin. Here, too, came Hongi and Ruatara, and having given them each a present of an axe or something useful, he asked them to make friends and promise to fight no more. Then to Marsden's great joy the rival chiefs fell upon each other's necks, rubbed noses (which is the Maori way of shaking hands), and so made peace. The Whangaroan chiefs then went away much pleased with their presents, and vowing always to love the missionaries, and never more to hurt British traders.

The Sunday after this meeting was Christmas Day and Ruatara was very anxious that there should be "church." So without telling anyone, he began to make great preparations.

First he fenced in about an acre of land. Then he made a pulpit and a reading-desk out of an old canoe, and covered them with black cloth. He also made seats for the white people out of bits of old canoes, and upon the highest point near he set up a flagstaff. Then having finished all his preparations he went to tell Mr. Marsden that everything was ready for a Christmas service.

So on Christmas morning 1815 the first Christmas service was held in New Zealand. Everyone from the ship, except one man and a boy, went ashore. For Marsden was so sure that the Maoris meant to be friendly that he felt there was no need for any one to stay to guard the ship.

The Union Jack was run up, and when Mr. Marsden landed he found the Maori chiefs drawn up in line ready to receive him. They were all dressed in regimentals which the Governor of New South Wales had given them, and behind them were gathered their whole tribes, men, women, and children. And thus, following the white men, they all marched to "church."

The white men took their seats, and behind them crowded the dark-faced savages. The ground was carpeted with green fern, the sky was blue above, and a very solemn silence fell upon the waiting crowd as Mr. Marsden and his friends stood up and sang the Old Hundredth Psalm.

All people that on earth do dwell,
Sing to the Lord with cheerful voice.
Him serve with mirth, His praise forth tell,
Come ye before Him and rejoice.
Know that the Lord is God indeed;
Without our aid He did us make:
We are His flock, He doth us feed,
And for His sheep He doth us take.

When the singing was over Marsden read the English Church Service. The people stood up and knelt down at a sign from one of their chiefs, for they understood not a word of what was said.

"We don't know what it all means," they said to Ruatara.

"Never mind," said he, "you will understand later."

"Behold I bring you glad tidings of great joy," was Marsden's text, and when the sermon was over Ruatara tried to explain in Maori language what it was all about. And if the Maoris did not quite understand all, this they did understand, that Mr. Marsden wanted to be kind to them, and bring peace between his countrymen and theirs.

CHAPTER III

HONGI THE WARRIOR

MR. MARSDEN could not stay long in New Zealand, for his work was in Australia. But there came with him two missionaries, and they stayed when he left. One of these missionaries taught the Maoris how to build houses and boats; the other taught how to make fishing-lines and other useful things. For Marsden did believe in teaching the savages only to be Christian. He thought it best to teach them first how to live decent and comfortable lives, and how to trade. "You cannot form a nation without trade and the civil arts," he said.

Before he left New Zealand Marsden bought about two hundred acres of land, paying twelve axes for it to the chief to whom it belonged. Upon this the missionaries built their houses and schools, and this was the first piece of land really possessed by the British in New Zealand, and their title to it was duly set down in writing. "Know all men to whom these shall come, that I, Anodee O Gunna, King of Ranghechoo, in the Island of New Zealand, have, for twelve axes to me in hand now paid and delivered by the Reverend Samuel Marsden, given, granted, bargained, and sold, all that parcel of land in the district of Hoshee, in the Island of New Zealand, for ever."

This writing was signed by two Englishmen, and as Gunna could not write, Hongi drew a copy of the tattooing on his face upon the parchment, and Gunna set his mark to it. Thus the white man first set his hand upon the land.

This bargain being settled, Marsden returned to Australia. He was gladly received by his friends there, for they had hardly hoped to see him return alive from the dreaded cannibal islands.

Although Samuel Marsden was a clergyman and wanted to make the Maoris Christian, he thought the best way of doing that was to teach them how to live better lives, how to plant wheat, build houses, and live in peace with their neighbours. "Hoes, spades and axes," he said, "are silent but sure missionaries."

So he encouraged them to trade. But one thing he would not sell to the Maoris. That thing was firearms. He sent a blacksmith to live among the heathen and teach them his trade. But he was forbidden to make or mend any weapon. No missionary was allowed to sell guns, and when Marsden discovered that one had disobeyed his orders he was sent away in disgrace.

But Hongi, although he had made peace at Marsden's bidding, was a fierce, proud warrior. He lived for revenge, and loved power. "There is but one king in Britain," he said, "and there shall be but one in New Zealand." He resolved that he should be that king. But before he began his conquests he paid a visit to England.

In England Hongi was feted and made much of. For it was almost as good as going to a wild beast show to dine with a cannibal chief. He became a "lion" and went from one fine house to another, being everywhere loaded with presents. Hongi saw many wonderful things, but he liked best to watch the soldiers and to wander among the arms and armour in the Tower.

Hongi went one day to see the king, and he, knowing his love for soldiers, gave him a suit of old armour. Of all the presents he received, Hongi prized his suit of armour most.

At last, his mind filled with all the splendours he had seen, Hongi sailed homeward. On his way he stopped ay Sydney, and there he sold all his fine presents, except only his armour. With the money he bought guns and ammunition, and once more set out for New Zealand.

Then Hongi began his career of conquest. None now could stand against him. Battle after battle was fought. Wooden spears went down before his thunder of guns, and after the battles the victors rejoiced in horrid revelry upon the bodies of their foes.

Thousands were slain, hundreds more men, women, and children were led captives as slaves. From end to end, North Island was filled with wrath and tears. Hongi stalked in conquering pride, glorying in the numbers he had killed and eaten.

The missionaries were in despair. All the good they had done, all Marsden's peacemaking, seemed to have been in vain. For six years the country was filled with slaughter and woe, and the beautiful fernland was turned into a desert, where men wandered seeking revenge and blood.

But at last Hongi's career of war and triumph came to an end. Other tribes saw that their only safety lay in getting guns to fight guns. And guns they got. And so the slaughter was made worse, until at length Hongi was wounded and died. He died a warrior, "*Kia toa, kia toa,*" he said, "be brave, be brave."

Hongi lived and died in the shedding of blood, yet he never harmed the missionaries. They were doers of good, he said. He was Marsden's friend, and he sent his children to the missionary schools, but he himself never became a Christian.

After Hongi's death the missionaries once more became peacemakers, and they persuaded the lawless tribes to lay down their weapons. But it was uphill work, for bad, white men were constantly undoing the good which the missionaries did. So battles, and murders, and horrid cannibal feasts went on.

Sometimes, too, without meaning it, white men made the Maoris angry. It was, for instance, a great crime to touch anything which, for some reason or another, had been declared to be "*tapu,*" that is sacred. White people did not understand the rules of *tapu*, and often in sheer ignorance they broke them. According to Maori law this was a sin which could only be wiped out by blood, so, often for seemingly harmless deeds, white men were horribly murdered.

Yet in spite of all dangers, in spite of the dark tales of horror, some settlers were at length lured to the shores. For the land was wonderfully fertile, and people hoped to make great fortunes. So a shipload of colonists arrived, determined to make their homes in New Zealand.

But just at this time the islanders were at war with each other, and soon after they landed the colonists saw a war dance. It was night time. Fires and flaring torches lit up the dusky forms of five or six hundred warriors, who stood in four long rows, swaying and stamping in time to the chant of their leader. With waving arms and rolling eyes they joined in chorus. Thrusting out their tongues, grinning horribly, in the flickering light they seemed like dancing demons. Now uttering loud yells, now hissing like a thousand serpents, now crashing their weapons together, they danced on. Bending, swaying, hissing, yelling, they went through all the actions of war, in fancy killing and eating their enemies. The sight was too much for the new-come colonists. Filled with horror and dread, they fled from the land as quickly as possible.

Yet in spite of all their wild savagery Marsden loved the Maoris. He returned again and again to visit them. Him they always greeted with joy; him they were always ready to obey. When for the last time he came among them he was an old white-haired man, unable to ride or walk far. But, glad to serve him, the Maoris carried him about in a litter, and when he spoke of trying to ride they were quite hurt. Soon after his last visit to New Zealand Marsden died, regretted and mourned by all who knew him, but by none so much as by the Maoris, who had lost in him a good friend.

CHAPTER IV

HOW THE MAORIS BECAME THE CHILDREN OF THE GREAT
WHITE QUEEN

ALTHOUGH it was now more than sixty years since Cook had planted the Union Jack and claimed the islands of New Zealand for the British Crown, they were not yet considered part of the British Empire. Many evil deeds were done in the islands by white men, and the British seemed to have no power, or no will to stop them. "The islands are not within His Majesty's dominions" was the convenient answer to all appeals for help.

But at last, in 1832, a British Resident was sent to live in New Zealand. He was told to try and make things better, but he had no power. He did nothing. He could do nothing. "A ship of war without any guns," he was scornfully called.

About this time Baron de Thierry, a Frenchman who had spent much of his life in England, tried to make himself King of New Zealand. He bought, or thought he bought, a great part of North Island for thirty axes. Then he issued proclamations calling himself, "Charles Baron de Thierry, Sovereign Chief of New Zealand, and King of Nuhuheva," and promising his protection and favour to all who would take office under him.

When the British Resident, Mr. Busby, saw this proclamation, he began to be afraid that the French were coming to take the land. So he banded thirty-five of the Maori chiefs together into what he called the United States of New Zealand. These chiefs declared themselves independent, but at the same time they begged the King of Great Britain to protect them against their enemies.

This declaration Busby sent to Thierry. But Thierry replied that New Zealand was not a British possession, that Tasman was there before Cook, and that he as king came to protect New Zealand liberties.

All this time Thierry had lived and written at a distance. Now he arrived in his kingdom. He brought with him only about ninety followers, gathered chiefly from the riff-raff of Sydney. He planted his flag, however, ordered his followers to stand bareheaded in his presence, and to be careful never to turn their backs when they left it. He scattered empty titles and honours around, and began to make a carriage drive from his "palace" to the Bay of Islands.

But the new king soon found that his thirty axes had only brought for him two or three hundred acres of land, instead of the kingdom he had thought. His money came to an end, his followers laughed at him, and his kingship ended in air.

A few years after this some people in England formed a company, which they called the New Zealand Land Company. Hundreds of acres of land were sold in London before it had been bought from the natives or even seen by any white man. Hundreds of people, eager to make money, bought this land without knowing anything about it, except that it was somewhere in New Zealand. Then the Company sent a shipload of settlers out to found a colony.

This was against the law, for, before a British colony can be formed, leave must be given from the crown. No such leave had been asked or given. Indeed the ship was sent off in secret.

Now at last the British Government woke up. It was seen that something must be done. On the one hand British settlers had to be protected from the cruelties of the Maoris. On the other hand the Maoris had to be protected from greedy, land-grabbing white people.

So Captain Hobson was sent out to be the first governor. He was told to make treaties with the native chiefs, and then to declare New Zealand to be a British colony.

On the 29th of February 1840 Hobson landed, and upon the 5th February he held a great meeting of the chiefs at a place called Waitangi.

On a plain near the town a platform was raised, and here at noon the governor took his seat, with the principal white people. Close round the platform sat the grave, dark-faced Maori chieftains, and behind them gathered the rest of the white people. The sun shone from a sky blue and cloudless, the gay tents of the British, decorated with flags, showed bravely against the background of waving trees. It was a scene of beauty and of peace. But there were those who shook their heads and sighed. No good would come of the meeting, they said, for did not Waitangi mean "weeping water"?

When all were gathered, Hobson spoke to the people. But as he could not speak the Maori language a missionary translated what he said to them. He told them how the great white Queen far over the sea loved all her people. He told them that if they would promise to be her children she would love them too. The great white Queen was very powerful, he said, and would protect them from all their enemies, if they would acknowledge her as their overlord.

When Hobson had finished, the Maori chiefs were asked to speak their thoughts. Many of them did not wish to make a treaty. "Send the man away," said one. "Do not sign the paper.

If you do you will become his slaves. Your land will be taken from you. You will no longer be chiefs, but will have to break stones upon the roads."

Then an old chief named Waka Nene rose. He was great in battle, wise in council, and his people listened to him willingly. Now he prayed them to hearken to the white lord. "You will be our father," he said, turning to Hobson. "You will not allow us to become slaves. You will keep our old customs, and never allow our land to be taken from us."

Then there was much talk this way and that. Many of the chiefs grew fierce and excited, others sat in sullen anger. At last it was agreed that they should think about it for one day and return then to tell the governor what they had decided.

Next day the treaty was signed. Waka Nene, the wise old warrior who had spoken so well, signed his name as the missionaries had taught him to do. The other chiefs made marks on the paper like the tattooing on their faces. A little later the treaty was signed by many of the chiefs on South Island, and by the end of June Victoria was proclaimed overlord of North and South Islands by treaty, and of Stewart Island by right of discovery. Thus New Zealand became part of the British Empire.

Soon after this the town of Auckland was founded and made the headquarters of the government. And now that New Zealand had become a British possession, people began to believe that the land would grow peaceful and safe to live in, and in a very short time hundreds of settlers arrived.

In the meantime, a town in the south of North Island had been founded by the New Zealand Company, who, you remember, had secretly sent off a shipload of colonists. They called their town Wellington, in honour of the great Duke.

Wakefield, the leader of the Company, had, by this time too, bought great tracts of land from the Maoris for such things as guns, razors, looking-glasses, sealing wax, nightcaps, jews' harps. Many of the Maoris did not understand the bargains. Many of them had no power to sell the land, and no wish to do so. They only pretended to do so because they wanted the guns and other things. Wakefield, on the other hand, had really no power to buy. For since Queen Victoria had become overlord, land could only be bought through the government. So trouble began. Indeed all the war and trouble there has been in New Zealand has arisen out of quarrels over land. Wakefield did not understand the Maoris, and knew nothing of their land laws, which were very difficult to follow. Sometimes both Maoris and white people would claim the same piece of ground, the one saying that he had bought it, the other saying that he had never sold it. And when the Maoris saw that the white people were taking all the best of the land they grew angry and frightened, and quarrels followed. So the new governor's task was not an easy one. But Hobson was a good and true man, and did his best to be fair both to Maoris and to white men.

Hobson worked hard in spite of illness, for soon after the signing of the Waitangi treaty he became ill. He never got well again, but in spite of that he stuck to his post bravely, until after two and a half years he died.

During these two and a half years New Zealand leaped forward as if by magic. When Hobson first came there were not two thousand white people in all the islands. When he died there were twelve thousand. Besides Auckland and Wellington, the towns of New Plymouth and Nelson, as well as many other villages, had sprung up. There were schools and churches, newspapers, soldiers, and police, where a few months before there had been only one or two missionaries, and wild traders, scattered amongst fierce man-eating savages.

The Maoris, as well as the white people, were sorry when Governor Hobson died. "Mother Victoria," wrote one of the chiefs to the Queen, "my subject is a Governor for us Maoris and for the Pakeha (settlers) in this island. Let him be a good man. Look out for a good man, a man of judgment. Let not a troubler come here. Let not a boy come here, or one puffed up. Let him be a good man as the Governor who has just died."

CHAPTER V

THE "HEAVENLY DAWN" AND THE "WILD CABBAGE LEAF"
MAKE WAR

"Rauparaha's war chant,
Rauparaha's fame song,
Rauparaha's story
Told on the harp-strings,
Pakeha harp-cords
Tuned by the stranger.

No wild hero of romance,
Born in dreamy poet's trance,
    Cradled in some mythic fane,
    Built up in a minstrel's brain
On imagination's plan!—
No such hero was this man.
    He was flesh and blood and bone,
    Standing forth erect, alone,
    High above his fellows known!—
Hist'ry paints what he hath done,
Maori valour's bravest son—
Te Rauparaha, Te Rauparaha!

Quick of eye and lithe of limb,
Warriors bent the knee to him!—
    Bold of heart, strong of hand,
    Formed to rule and to command

Suckled on a breast that gave
Milk of heroes to the brave!—
        Richest fruit of Toa's seed,
        Scion of heroic breed,
        Born to conquer and to lead!
Strongest branch of noblest tree
From Hawaiki o'er the sea,
Te Rauparaha, Te Rauparaha!"

THOMAS BRACKEN.

AFTER the signing of the treaty of Waitangi the Maoris lived in peace with the white people. The only quarrels were about land, but these were bitter indeed.

In the north of South Island there lay a beautiful valley called Wairau. This valley Colonel Wakefield claimed; but the chiefs, Rauparaha (the Wild Cabbage Leaf) and Rangihaeata (the Heavenly Dawn), to whom it belonged, declared that he had no right to it. "We have never sold it," they said. "And we never will sell it. We want it for our sons and their sons for ever. If you want our land you will have to kill us first, or make us slaves."

But Colonel Wakefield paid no attention to what the chiefs said. He called Rauparaha an old savage, and vowed soon to put an end to his rule. This, too, in spite of the treaty of Waitangi, by which the white men had promised to protect the Maoris.

Bent on having his own way, Wakefield sent men to mark out the valley of Wairau for farms. But Rauparaha and his followers turned the men off. They were quite polite and gentle about it, but quite firm. They did no harm to any of the white men, or to their belongings. They simply carried all their instruments and tools to their boats and left them there. Next the Maoris pulled up all the flags and stakes with which the land had been marked out, and burned them. They burned the huts which the white men had built, too. "I have the right to do this," said Rauparaha, "for they were built of wood grown upon my own land. So they are mine."

Very angry were Wakefield's men when they returned to Nelson. There they went to the magistrate and told him of the treatment they had received. From him they got a letter or warrant to take Rauparaha and Rangihaeata prisoner, for having burned their houses.

Armed with this warrant they went back to Wairau, accompanied by the magistrate and some workmen. Workmen and gentlemen together, they numbered about fifty; only about thirty-five of them, however, had guns. But even so they thought they would be a match for any number of savages.

When they came to the mouth of the Wairau river, however, they were met by a Christian chief. He warned them to be careful what they did. But they would not listen, and marched on up the river, until they came to where Rauparaha was encamped on the other side.

A few of the party boldly crossed the stream and asked for Rauparaha.

"Here I am," he said, rising, "what do you want?"

"You must come with me, to Nelson," said the magistrate, "because you have burned a house, which you had no right to do."

"I will not go," replied the Wild Cabbage Leaf.

"But you must," said the magistrate. "I have brought the Queen's book," he added, showing him the warrant, "that says you must go."

Then Rangihaeata sprang up. He was tall and handsome, his dark face was fierce with pride and anger. Behind him stood his wife Te Ronga, the daughter of Rauparaha. "Are we not in our own land?" he cried angrily. "We do not go to England to interfere with you. Leave us alone."

And so the quarrel waxed, and angry words were bandied back and forth. A pair of handcuffs were brought out. Rauparaha put his hands under his cloak and cried again that he would not go to be a slave.

Then from among the white people a shot was fired. It struck Te Ronga where she stood beside her husband, and she fell dying to the ground.

In a moment all was wild confusion. Volley after volley was fired. "Farewell the light! Farewell the day! Welcome the darkness of death!" cried Rauparaha.

Before the wild charge of the Maoris the British fled. A few stood their ground, but at last, seeing resistance useless, they waved a handkerchief to show that they surrendered.

Rauparaha then ordered his followers to cease fighting. But Rangihaeata was mad with sorrow and hatred. "Do not forget that they slew your daughter, Te Ronga!" he cried, and the unresisting Britons were slain where they stood. In all, twenty-two were killed: the rest, some of them sorely wounded, escaped.

As soon as the heat of fight was over Rauparaha began to fear the white man's vengeance. He had few followers in South Island, so, taking to his canoes, he and they rowed over Cook's strait to North Island, where his tribe lived.

The weather was stormy, and the waves dashed over the canoes as they sped along. But the Maoris were the vikings of the south. Little they cared for the dangers of the deep, for their hearts were hot within them, and as they bent to the oars they sang, their wild voices rising above the roar of the storm.

Wet and weary, Rauparaha landed, and with the salt spray still on his lips, with the song of the storm wind still in his ear, he spoke to his countrymen. Such wild, stirring words he spoke that they were ready to rise and sweep the white man into the sea.

"Now is the time to strike!" he cried. "Now we know what the smooth talk of the Pakeha is worth. You know now what they mean in their hearts. You know now that you can wait for nothing but tyranny at their hands. Come, sweep them from the land that they would water with our blood." And as Rauparaha spoke, he jangled the insulting handcuffs in the ears of his people.

Fortunately there were white men in New Zealand who both knew and loved the Maoris. They soothed the hurt and angry souls of the savages, and the white men, who had begun the quarrel, were told that what they had done was "unlawful, unjust and unwise."

When the new governor, Captain Robert Fitzroy, arrived in New Zealand, he went to see Rauparaha and Rangihaeata, and heard from themselves the story of their wrongs. He listened to all that they had to say, then he told the Maoris that they had committed a great crime in killing men who had surrendered, but because the white men were wrong in the beginning he would not punish them for their deaths. In this way peace was made. But many of the white men were angry that the blood of their brothers had not been avenged. Some of them were so angry that they wrote home and asked that this new governor, who so favoured the Maoris, should be called home again.

CHAPTER VI

THE FLAGSTAFF WAR

BESIDES the land troubles others now beset the governor. After New Zealand became a British colony many changes followed. Gradually the unseen power of Civilisation laid hold upon the islands. The chiefs began to feel uneasy. Something, they knew not what, was rising up around them. Somehow their power was vanishing. Old customs were slipping away. New and strange ones were coming into use. The people were made to pay taxes, a thing they found hard to understand. Ships coming to New Zealand ports had to pay custom duties before landing their goods. So tobacco and blankets grew dear, whale ships almost ceased to come to the Bay of Islands, where once they had crowded, and the trade of the town Kororarika was almost ruined.

A vague fear and discontent spread among the people. Then there were not wanting base white people who pointed to the British flag, and told the dark chieftains that there lay the cause of all their sorrows. And so the idea took root that if only that flag were removed the good old days would return again.

Near Kororarika, on the Bay of Islands, there lived a young chief called Honi Heke. He had married the daughter of the great chief Hongi, and, like him, longed to be powerful among his people. He was restless and clever, and he hated the white people. He was no ignorant savage, for the missionaries had taught him much. But although at one time he became a Christian, later he turned back to his heathen ways.

Proud, wild, and discontented Heke was ready to fight any one. And when one day a woman of his tribe, who had married a white man, called him a pig, he gathered around him a hundred hot-headed young savages like himself, and marching into Kororarika, he plundered the white man's house, and carried off his wife. Then having danced a war-dance, he and his followers cut down the flagstaff, from which floated the Union Jack, and departed rejoicing.

This was serious, and the governor resolved to put an end to Heke's wild tricks. But in all New Zealand there were not ninety soldiers. So he sent to Australia begging for help. Sir George Gipps, the Governor of New South Wales, at once sent a shipload of men and guns. But before they came, Waka Nene and some other friendly chiefs begged Fitzroy not to fight.

"We will guard the flagstaff," they said. "We are old folks and faithful. We will make the young folks be faithful too."

Then at a great meeting twenty-five chiefs apologised for Heke's behaviour, but he himself did not come. Instead he wrote a letter which was only half an apology, for he said the flagstaff was his own. It had been brought, he said, from the forest by his own people, and had been meant, not for the British flag, but for the flag of New Zealand.

However, Fitzroy accepted the apology such as it was. The chiefs, in token of their submission, laid their guns at his feet. He gave them back again making a long speech, in which he warned the Maoris not to believe or be led astray by the tales of wicked white men.

After this, Governor Fitzroy took away the custom duties and made Kororarika a free port once more. He hoped in this way to bring wealth and trade to the town again, and make the people more contented. And when they heard the news, the white settlers were so glad that they used up all the candles in the town to make an illumination to show their joy. So peace was once more made. The soldiers were sent away, a new flagstaff was set up, and again the Union Jack floated out on the breeze.

But before many months had gone Heke once more gathered his men, and the flagstaff was cut down a second time. Heke hated it as the sign that the Maoris had no more power in the land. "God made this land for us and for our children!" he cried. "Are we the only people that God has made without a land to live upon?"

Again Governor Fitzroy sent to Sydney for help. He also offered a reward of £100 to any one who would bring Heke prisoner to him.

This made Heke's followers very angry. "Is Heke a pig," they asked, "that he should be bought and sold?" And he in his turn offered £100 for the governor's head.

Again two hundred soldiers came from New South Wales. Again the flagstaff was set up. And this time it was hooped and barred with iron, and a blockhouse was built near in which a guard was stationed.

All this made the Maoris more sure than ever that the flagstaff was really the cause of their troubles. "See," they said, "the flagstaff does mean power, or why should the Pakehas set it up again and guard it so carefully!"

All the wild and discontented young men now gathered to Heke, who had sworn the downfall of the flagstaff, and of the power of which it was the sign.

It was in vain that the missionaries, who had always been peacemakers, tried to make peace now. Printed copies of the Waitangi treaty were sent to the Maori rebels. But Heke would neither listen nor give in. "It is all soap," he said, "very smooth and oily, but treachery is hidden at the bottom of it." One Sunday morning a missionary went to his camp to preach. His text was, "Whence come wars and fightings." Heke listened to it quietly, then he said, "Go, speak that sermon to the British, they need it more than we."

Days went on, and still the Union Jack floated from the hill above the town. Still Heke and his men lay encamped near, breathing defiance. The people of Kororarika, well knowing that Heke never broke his word, began to drill, and prepared to give him a hot welcome when he came. But in the end he took them unawares. One morning in March, before the sun was up, two hundred men came creeping, creeping up the hill. The guard was taken by surprise. Before the officer in charge knew what was happening, the enemy were in possession of the blockhouse, and the soldiers were being driven downhill.

Then the axes went to work, and for the third time the flagstaff fell.

The townspeople armed themselves, and with the soldiers and marines from the warship which lay in the bay, defended themselves right bravely. But the Maoris had the best position on the flagstaff hill, and after hours of fighting, men, women, and children fled to the ship, leaving their town to the mercy of the foe.

Great was the joy of the savages when they saw the white folk go. They danced, and sang, and made grand speeches. Then dashing upon the town they began to plunder it.

As the fighting was now stopped, many of the people ventured back again in the hope of saving some of their goods. The Maoris were now perfectly good natured, and did not try to hurt them. Then might be seen the strange sight of Maori and white man carrying off goods from the same house, the one trying to save his own, the other taking whatever he had a mind to take. But before long fire broke out. It raged among the wooden buildings, and Kororarika was soon little more than a blackened ruin.

Homeless and penniless, many of them having nothing left to them but the clothes they wore, the settlers fled to Auckland. Here something like a panic seized hold of the people. Many of them sold their farms for almost nothing and fled from the land in terror.

But the Maoris followed their victory by no cannibal feast. Instead they allowed the missionaries to bury the dead. They even helped some women and children who had been left behind to join their friends. Indeed through all the war the British could not but admire the courteous, generous behaviour of their savage foes.

CHAPTER VII

THE WARPATH

"When will your valour begin to rage?
When will your valour be strong?
Ah! when the tide murmurs,
Ah! when the tide roars.
Bid farewell to your children,
For what more can you do?
You see how the braves are coming amain,
Like the lofty exulting peaks of the hills,
They yield, they yield! O Fame!"

MAORI WAR-SONG.

HEKE'S fame spread far and wide. He boasted of the defeat of the white men, and threatened that when the moon was full he would attack Auckland and sweep it from the earth, as he had swept Kororarika. All the colony was shaken with fear. Everywhere towns were fortified. Everywhere settlers drilled, and practised, and made ready for war.

The governor saw that he must now fight in good earnest. For only after Heke was subdued could there be peace. So again he sent to Australia for soldiers. Meanwhile Waka Nene and the friendly Maoris helped the British, and took up arms against their lawless countrymen.

After the sack of Kororarika, Heke and his warriors marched

away to a strong, native fortress or "pah" called Okaihau. There Waka Nene followed him, and there he was joined later by a British force under Colonel Hume.

When the British soldiers arrived they were very much astonished at sight of their allies. Was it possible, they asked, that they were expected to fight side by side with a rabble of half-naked savages? Their astonishment became still greater when the Maoris, in their honour, danced a war-dance, which Waka Nene's wife led, and in which Waka Nene himself joined, dressed in the uniform of a British officer.

It was May when the troops landed. But May in New Zealand is like November at home. The weather was cold and wet. For four days the men marched through almost pathless forest, under torrents of rain. The way was so bad that no baggage-wagons could pass along it. So the men had neither tents nor proper food. Each man carried his own biscuits and slept upon the damp ground. Thus wearied and hungry, they arrived before Heke's pah.

Between a large lake and a wooded hill lay the fortress. It was built of two rows of tree-trunks twelve feet high, and so closely set together that only the barrel of a gun could pass between. The outer fence was covered with flax, and between the two was a deep ditch. Without cannon it was impossible to take such a fort, and the British had only a rocket-tube.

The British began their attack by firing their rockets. The first struck away a strong post, burst inside the pah, and frightened the defenders so much that some of them were ready to flee. But no one being hurt they took courage again. Then as rocket after rocket fell wide of the mark, they watched them with surprise and scorn. "What prize can be won by such a gun?" they sneered, and they were no longer afraid.

Presently they gained so much courage that they came out of their pah to fight. But the British soldiers charged them with fixed bayonets and drove them back again.

So for many hours the fight lasted, the Maoris firing in safety from behind their strong palisade, against which the British vainly wasted their shot. Lead whistled through the air in all directions, the whole country seemed on fire, "and brave men worked their work."

At length the fighting ceased and both sides retired to rest. As the British soldiers sat round their camp-fires they heard a strange sound coming from the Maori pah. the sound of singing. Plaintive and wailing it rose and fell in the still air. It was the Maoris singing their evening hymn. "Fight and pray," had said their priests. "Touch not the spoils of the slain, eat not of human flesh lest the God of the missionaries should be angry. And be careful not to offend the Maori gods. It is good to have more than one God to trust to. Be brave, be strong, be patient." So ignorant and simple, trusting in they knew not what, the Maoris now sang a hymn to the God of the missionaries.

Next day, seeing how hopeless it was to try to take the fort without cannon, Hume marched his soldiers away.

The people in Auckland had been eagerly awaiting the news that Heke was captured. And when instead of that news the worn-out, haggard troops reached the town, they were struck with dismay. Was it possible that two hundred and fifty savages had been more than a match for four hundred well-trained British soldiers? It was the second time that the Maoris had beaten "the wearers of red garments," and now the British began to tremble for their hold on the land.

Meanwhile Heke swaggered about in the glory of victory. He wrote letters to the governor which were about peace indeed, but which breathed war in every line.

More soldiers, however, now arrived from Australia under Colonel Despard. They brought with them four cannon, and the colonists began to feel more cheerful.

The last fight had taught Heke that in the open his soldiers could not stand against British soldiers. He had learned that his safety was in the strength of his fortresses. So now he retired to a pah called Oheawai, which was far stronger than Okaihau.

Here the British resolved to attack him. But it was with great difficulty that the cannon were brought along the rugged path through the forest to Heke's camp, for they were ship's guns, and the wheels were only fifteen inches high. Many a time they stuck fast in the marshy forest, but the friendly Maoris harnessed themselves to the carriages, and at length all difficulties were passed, and in the dusk of a winter's evening the whole army encamped before Heke's fort.

That night there was little sleep in either camp. Through the night as they lay awake on the ground, the British soldiers heard the Maoris in their pah praying, singing, and talking.

In the morning the fight began. The great cannon-balls crashed and crashed against the huge, wooden walls without doing much damage. And when all the heavy ammunition was done only a small breach had been made. But small though it was, Colonel Despard, against the advice of his officers and of the friendly Maoris, ordered a party to storm it.

Bravely the soldiers obeyed his orders. Shouting their war-cry, they charged the breach. Bravely they fought and fell. The breach was narrow. It was defended by hundreds of well-armed Maoris. Fighting valiantly, the British passed the outer fence; but the inner fence was still unbroken. From it a hail of bullets blazed upon the gallant stormers, and man after man went down.

After ten minutes of awful slaughter and confusion the British fell back, leaving half their number dead upon the ground.

Then followed a night of horror. The dead and dying lay untended round the pah. Through the still night air the groans of the wounded were heard, mingled with the songs of triumph sung by the exulting savages.

"SHOUTING THEIR WAR CRY, THE BRITISH CHARGED THE BREACH."

"O Youth of sinewy force,
O man of martial strength,
Behold the sign of power!
In my hand I hold the scalp
Of the Kawau Tatakaha."

Often too, through the night the watch-cry of the pah was heard. "Come on! Come on! soldiers for revenge. Come on! Stiff lie your dead by the fence of my pah. Come on, come on!"

Round their camp-fires the British sat wakeful, watchful, downcast, eating their hearts out in anger and despair.

For two days there was little fighting. The Maoris hung out a flag of truce and told the British they might bury their dead. Then more ammunition having arrived for the great guns, the bombardment again began. Soon the breach already made became much larger, and a second assault was planned.

When morning dawned the pah was to be taken. But during the night the Maoris, seeing they could hold their fortress no longer, slipped quietly away to the forest, leaving their empty pah to the British. So quietly did they go that the British knew nothing about it until they were told by a friend that the Maoris were already ten miles away.

It was hard to fight such a slippery foe. It was useless to try to follow them into the forest wilds, so Colonel Despard marched his men away to Kororarika to rest. And the governor, hoping that now Heke might be persuaded to make peace, told him not to fight any more for the present.

CHAPTER VIII

THE STORMING OF THE BAT'S NEST

HEKE was yet far from making peace. He and his friends in their new fastness at Ikorangi were dancing the war-dance, and singing songs of exultation—

> "An attack! an attack! E ha!
> A battle! a battle! E ha!
> A fight on the banks of the river.
> It is completely swept and emptied.
> O you would fight, you would fight.
> You had better stayed at home in Europe
> Than have suffered a repulse from Whareahau.
> He has driven you back to your God.
> You may cast your book behind,
> And leave your religion on the ground.
> An attack! an attack! E ha!
> A battle! a battle! E ha!"

Heke's fame grew greater and greater, for had he not twice defeated "the wearers of red garments." Peace was far from his thoughts, and Governor Fitzroy was about to attack him again, when he was recalled. The British Government were not pleased at the way in which the colony was drifting into war, and Captain George Grey was sent to take Fitzroy's place.

Captain Grey made up his mind to have no more fighting if that were possible. He sent messengers to the rebel chiefs, saying that if they would yield before a certain date, they would be pardoned, and that if they had been in any way wronged, they should have justice.

But Heke would not yield, and once more the war began. This time the Maori forces were divided. Heke was at Ikorangi, and his friend Kawiti at Ruapekapeka, the Bat's Nest. It was upon the Bat's Nest that the attack was made. It was a pah like Oheawai and Okaihau, but far stronger than either. For between the huge wooden fences there was a great mud wall against which cannon balls were of little use.

The British force was now much stronger than before. They had more and heavier guns, but still for days the bombardment went on with little result. Then one day Heke arrived to join his friends, bringing many more warriors with him. The next day being Sunday, the Maoris thought there would be no fighting, for the missionaries had taught them to keep it as a day of rest. So they all gathered in the outworks for prayer, leaving the fort almost unguarded.

The British, however, had no thought of keeping Sunday. A friendly Maori, seeing how quiet it was within the pah, crept close up to the walls. Finding them unguarded, he made signs to the British. Quickly they charged, and before the Maoris realised what was happening, the red-coats had possession of the fort.

Now the very strength of the pah was turned against the Maoris. Secure behind the massive ramparts, the British fired upon the foe. A fierce fight followed. But to dislodge the British from their strong position was impossible, and at last the Maoris fled to the woods.

Tired of the fight, the followers of Heke and Kawiti now scattered and fled. They had little food left; starvation and death stared them in the face.

"Can shadows carry muskets?" they said. And so the army melted away. In a few days Heke and Kawiti found themselves almost alone. The end had come. At last the proud chieftains sued for peace.

"Friend Governor, let peace be made between you and me," wrote Kawiti. "I have had enough of your cannon-balls, therefore I say let us make peace. Will you not? Yes. This is the end of my war against you. Friend Governor, I, Kawiti and Heke, do consent to this good message. It is finished."

Now that the rebel chiefs were in his power. Sir George was merciful. He pardoned all who had taken part in the rebellion, and allowed them to remain in possession of their lands. But Heke's proud, restless spirit could not bear the bonds of peace. He pined away, and died at the age of forty-two. As for his old friend Kawiti, he lived to the age of eighty, and then died of measles, a new disease brought into the country by the white men.

There were many who thought that Governor Grey had been too gentle with Heke and Kawiti and the other rebels. Many thought that they ought to have been punished. But time showed that Sir George was right, for the peace was lasting, and left no bitterness behind. Not while Heke or Kawiti lived, however, was the flagstaff at Kororarika put up again. But in 1857 Kawiti's son led four hundred of his people to the spot, and in token of friendship they raised a new flagstaff. They called it Whakakotahitanga, which means "being in union," and to this day the Union Jack floats from it.

CHAPTER IX

THE TAMING OF THE WILD CABBAGE LEAF

WHILE the north was at length settling down to peace, the tribes in the south were growing restless. Their leaders were, as before, Rauparaha the proud "Wild Cabbage Leaf," and Rangihaeata "The Heavenly Dawn." But while the Heavenly Dawn openly showed that he was an enemy, the Wild Cabbage Leaf pretended to be a friend to the British.

Land again was the beginning of the quarrel. About nine miles from Wellington was the fertile Hutt Valley. This Colonel Wakefield thought he had bought. The chiefs said it was still theirs, and they tried to prevent settlers taking possession of it, and soon the land was once more filled with fighting and murder.

So, having made peace in the north, Governor Grey sailed to Wellington, taking with him all the soldiers he could gather.

Soon he discovered that although Rauparaha made great show of friendship, he was really egging Rangihaeata on. In fact, while Rangihaeata was the fighter, Rauparaha was the thinker. So it was resolved to seize him and stop his mischief.

One night a company of a hundred and fifty men silently surrounded the chiefs house. All was quiet. Swiftly and stealthily the men stole into Rauparaha's room, and, while he was still sleeping, seized him. Not a blow was struck, not a shot was fired. The wily old chief was taken prisoner without a drop of blood being shed. But it was not done without a struggle, for Rauparaha bit and kicked fiercely, and his captors carried the marks of his teeth and nails for many a day.

Great was the grief of the Heavenly Dawn when he heard of the capture of his father-in-law. In his grief he made a lament, mourning for Rauparaha as for a dead man.

> "Raha! my chief, my friend,
> Thy lonely journey wend;
> Stand with thy wrongs before the God of Battles' face:
> Bid him thy woes requite.
> Ah me! Te Raukawa's foul desertion and disgrace,
> Ah me! the English ruler's might.
>
> Raha! my chief of chiefs,
> Ascend with all thy griefs
> Up to the Lord of Peace; there stand before his face:
> Let him thy fate requite.
> Ah me! Te Toa's sad defection and disgrace,
> Ah me! the English ruler's might."

But Rangihaeata did more than idly lament. Gathering his men, he prepared to avenge the capture of his chief. He wrote, too, to the northern tribes, stirring them to battle. "Friends and children, come and avenge the wrongs of Te Rauparaha, because Te Rauparaha is the eye of the faith of all men. Make ye haste hither in the days of December."

But the northern chiefs were slow to move. They told the Heavenly Dawn that it was folly to try to kill the British or drive them from the land. "How could you dry up the sea?" they asked.

But although few joined him, Rangihaeata fought. Although soldiers, sailors, settlers, all were against him, he would not give in. Defeated and hunted he took refuge, as he himself said, "in the fastnesses and hollows of the country, as a crab lies concealed in the depths and hollows of the rocks."

At length, left almost without a follower, Rangihaeata made peace. But his proud spirit never quite gave in. "I am not tired of war," he told Sir George Grey, "but the spirit of the times is for peace. Now, men, like women, use their tongues as weapons. Do not suppose, O Governor, that you have conquered me! No. It was my own relations and friends. It was by them I was overcome."

When Rauparaha had been seized he had been sent to Auckland. There, although he was a prisoner, he was allowed to go about freely. Now, when peace was come again, he was permitted to go home. But the fierce old chief did not live long to enjoy his liberty. Eighteen months later he died.

From first to last, in north and south, the war had lasted for five years. It had cost a million of money.

Sir George now had time to think of ruling the land. He tried to govern well and be just to the Maoris. He protected them as much as he could from land-grabbers, and kept the treaty of Waitangi. He rewarded those who had helped him, and in every way treated them fairly.

One good thing which Sir George did was to make good roads throughout the islands. Even while the war was going on, parties of soldiers and Maoris might be seen peacefully working side by side with pick and spade. The Maoris were good workmen, and the British soon grew friendly with them. They taught the Maoris English, and the Maoris taught them their language. And when the road was finished they parted like old friends.

Then Governor Grey built schools and had the Maori children taught to speak English, and did many other things for their happiness. So when in 1853 another governor was appointed, the Maoris were very sorrowful. They grieved for Sir George as for a lost father, and sang mournful songs of farewell.

"Oh then!
Pause for one moment there.
Cast back one glance on me,
Thus to receive one fond,
One last, fond look.
Thy love came first, not mine;
Thou didst first behold
With favour and regard
The meanest of our race!

Thence is it
The heart o'erflows;
the eye Bedewed with tears doth anxiously desire
To catch one fond, one parting glance,
Ere thou art lost to sight for ever,
    Alas! for ever!"

When Sir George Grey came home, too, he was welcomed and thanked. And when at Oxford he received a degree in honour of his work in New Zealand, the students gave three cheers for the "King of the Cannibal Islands."

CHAPTER X

THE KING OF THE MAORIS

THE colony of New Zealand grew rapidly greater and stronger. In 1847 Dunedin was founded by a party of Scottish settlers sent out by the Free Church of Scotland. In 1850 Canterbury was founded by the Church of England. These towns would have grown faster than they did, had not gold been discovered in Australia. For many then who had come from home, meaning to settle in New Zealand, rushed away to Australia and the gold diggings.

But things soon righted themselves, for it was not long before the fame of the grassy plains of New Zealand spread to Australia. Farmers there, hearing of these plains where not even a tree had to be cut down to clear the land, sailed over from Australia, bringing flocks with them. Soon the Canterbury pastures became as famous the world over as those of Australia. And since ways of keeping meat by freezing it have been found out, much of the mutton used in Great Britain is brought from New Zealand.

In 1852 New Zealand became a self-governing colony, and in 1854 the first New Zealand Parliament was held.

All seemed prosperous and well with the colony when once more land troubles began.

Some of the Maori chiefs had always been against selling

land to the British. "The money the white man gives is soon spent," they said. "The land is gone from us for ever, and we have nothing left." Yet, year by year they saw the white people fence in more and more land for farms. So now many of these tribes banded themselves together into a Land League. The members of this league vowed to sell no more land to the white people.

About this same time too, some of the tribes made up their minds to choose a king. In choosing this king they had no thought of rebelling against the Queen. But they saw that although the governor ruled the white men and the Maoris too, when they quarrelled with the white men, they let them fight amongst themselves as much as they liked. So they desired a king who should rule the Maoris as the Queen far away ruled her people. Within the large tract of land which they had vowed never to sell, the Maori king should rule alone. Within this land no road should be made—for all roads led to slavery.

There was much talk and argument before a king was chosen. For all did not agree that a king would be good to have. But at last a brave old warrior called Te Whero-Whero Potatau was elected. A standard, too, was chosen and raised. It was a white flag with a red border, bearing two red crosses, and the words "Potatau, King of New Zealand."

But many were against the flag, as they had been against the king. "I am content with the flag of Britain," said one old warrior. "It is seen all over the world. It belongs to me. I get some of its honour. What honour can I get from your flag? It is as a fountain without water."

"Let the flag stand," said another, "but wash out the writing upon it. As for me I am a subject of the Queen."

But in spite of all objections the flag was unfurled, the king was chosen.

Potatau was now treated with royal honours. Salutes were fired, his subjects stood bareheaded before him, and backed out of his presence, while he, wrapped in an old blanket, sat upon a mat and smoked his pipe.

And sometimes while his counsellors talked and made laws, he slept peacefully, knowing not what was done.

Governor Browne paid little attention to the "King movement" as it was called. If he had, he might have turned it to good. As it was, it turned to evil.

Soon a quarrel arose which led to fighting. A Maori offered to sell to the governor some land at Waitara, not far from New Plymouth. The governor bought it, but Te Rangitake, the chief in whose country the land was, being among those who had joined the Land League, forbade the sale. "I will not give it up!" he cried; "I will not, I will not, I will not! I have spoken."

The Maori land laws were very difficult for a white man to follow. The chiefs often had a kind of feudal right over the land, and so, although it did not really belong to Te Rangitake, he had a right to forbid the sale. "These lands will not be given by us into your hands," he wrote to Governor Browne, "lest we become like the birds of the sea which are resting upon a rock. When the tide flows the rock is covered by the sea. The birds fly away because there is no resting-place for them. I will not give you the land."

But the governor decided that Te Rangitake had no right to hinder the selling of the land. So he sent men to mark it out for farms. But the men were met by all the oldest and ugliest women in the land, who hugged and kissed them till they were obliged to run away.

Then the governor sent soldiers, and seeing that peaceful means were no longer of use, the whole tribe rose in arms. Rangitake built a pah upon the land, pulled up the governor's stakes and flags and burned them, and war began.

Once more the governor sent to Australia for soldiers. Once more the land was filled with blood and war.

From pah to pah the Maoris flitted as their custom was. Settlers in terror fled from their farms, leaving their homes, their flocks and herds, to the mercy of the Maoris. Some fled from the country altogether.

At first this quarrel had nothing to do with the King movement. Indeed Te Rangitake had refused to join that. But now the king tribes came to help their fellow countrymen. The king himself was old and feeble, so the men were led by a young and warlike chief called Te Waharoa. It was he, indeed, who had been one of the principal upholders of the king, and he was called the king-maker.

In the midst of all the trouble the king died, and his son Tawhiao was chosen in his stead. But he had not the fame of his father, and had little power among the natives.

For many months the war went on, but at length, in May 1861, peace was made, the governor promising to look into Te Rangitake's claims once more.

CHAPTER XI

TO THE SOUND OF THE WAR-SONG

THE peace was a mere truce. Things seemed drifting again to war when the government at home recalled Browne, and sent back Sir George Grey, who had already proved so good a ruler.

Sir George Grey, when he came, decided that the land at Waitara had been unjustly taken, and must be given back. But it was now too late. Misunderstandings and blunders grew worse and worse, and the second Maori war broke out. From India and from Australia, troops came to help the settlers, while the Maori tribes gathered to the sound of an old war-song.

Soon the fight began. The Maoris fought well and fiercely. It was the story of Oheawai and of the Bat's Nest over again. In a night the Maoris would build a fort strong enough to keep the British for a month at bay.

For days they would defend it, and when it seemed about to be taken would forsake it and flee to another as strong or stronger. They were always far outnumbered by the white men. Yet never once did the white men gain a great victory.

It seemed of little use to capture or destroy a pah, for the Maoris fled to another a few miles off, where the attack had to be begun afresh. The whole country seemed dotted with strong fortresses.

But at length at Rangiriri, a strong fort surrounded by a river and by swamps, many of the Maoris were captured. From dawn to dark on a wintry July day the thunder of war lasted. Shot and shell were poured upon the fort from every side. Again and again the British soldiers dashed at the walls, only to be thrown back again like waves broken upon a rock. But when night fell, the fort was completely surrounded. And when day dawned the Maoris hung out a flag and surrendered.

Governor Grey would have been glad now to make peace. But his advisers would not listen. So still the war went on.

At Orakau, one of the bravest defences of the war took place. Here two or three hundred badly-armed, half-starving Maori men and women bid defiance to more than fifteen thousand British soldiers.

After trying in vain to storm the fort, the British leader resolved to mine it and blow it up. But he knew that both women and children were within the pah. He wished to save them, so he sent a messenger with a flag of truce, asking them to surrender.

"We will fight to the end, for ever and ever," was the reply.

"Then send out the women and the children," said the messenger.

"Nay, the women and children, too, will fight," they cried.

So, worn with fight and watching, weary, hungry and thirsty, the Maoris still fought on. They had no food, they had no water, their shot was almost done. Yet they would not yield.

Then in their need they turned to the Christian God. He would help them. And through the crash and roar of cannon, the plaintive notes of a hymn arose. They looked to heaven, but from the once clear sky now darkened with the heavy clouds of war, no help came.

Then fiercer, wilder thoughts laid hold of the Maoris. The Christian God was the God of deceivers, they cried. He was the God of those who sought to rob them of their land. They would have no more of Him. They would turn again for help to their ancient god of War. Then fierce and loud above the clangour rose the sounds of a "Karakia," a chant of curses, a chant long unheard in Maori land.

Now the mines began to burst all around them. In noise and flame their pah was shattered. The earth shook with death. No longer could they hold the fortress.

Then, still chanting their wild and terrible song, under the eyes of the British, they marched calmly and steadily out of their fort. "As cool and steady as if going to church," said one who saw.

For some minutes all watched in wonder. No one knew what was happening. Then, "They are escaping! they are escaping!" came the cry, and the chase began.

For six long miles the way was red with blood, and strewn with dead. Yet steadily onward the Maoris pressed, now pausing to fire, now to lift a wounded comrade, until at last a broken remnant reached the wild refuge of the hills, where no white man could follow.

The war was nearly over. But at a place called the Gate Pah, the Maoris once more beat back the British troops, who fled, leaving ten officers and twenty-five men dead upon the field.

But again, in the darkness of the night, the Maoris slipped away. How they went no man knew, for the pah was surrounded by British troops. Only in the morning it was found that the pah was empty. And yet they had gone in no wild haste, for beside each wounded British soldier was a cup of water, placed there by the Maoris before they fled.

Only a few miles off the Maoris again made a stand. But here they were attacked before they had time to build a pah. After a desperate fight they fled.

Among the dead lay their leader. On his dead body was found the order for the day. It began with a prayer, and ended with the words, "If thine enemy hunger, feed him; if he thirst, give him drink."

"Te Waru was there with the East Coast braves,
And the chiefs famed in song and story,
Met on the spot to resist the spoilers,
Who had taken the land from the Maori
In the name of the Queen of the far land.
Only three hundred warriors were there
Entrenched within the weak unfinished pah,
Only three hundred brave men and women
To meet the Pakeha who surrounded
The sod-built fortress, with his well-drilled troops
Nearly two thousand hardy Britons.

Three hundred lion-hearted warriors
Assembled with Rewi to fan the flame
Of deadly hatred to the Pakeha
Into a vengeful blaze at Orakau,
Chanting the deeds of their ancestors,
They cried aloud, "Me mate te gangatu,
Me mate mo te whenua!" which means,
'The warrior's death is to die for the land.'

.   .   .   .   .

Then Major Mair, with flag of truce, before the Maoris stood,
And said, "O friends, be warned in time, we do not seek your blood.
Surrender, and your lives are safe." Then, through the whole redoubt,
The swarthy rebels answered, with a fierce, defiant shout,
"Ka whawkia tonu! Ake! ake! ake!"[1]

Again spake gallant Mair, "O friends, you wish for blood and strife,
With blind and stubborn bravery, preferring death to life;
But send your women and your children forth, they shall be free."
They answered back, "Our women brave will fight as well as we."

Again the fiery-throated cannon roared aloud for blood,
Again the hungry eagle swooped and shrieked aloud for food;
Again wild spirits soaring, saw their shattered shells beneath
In pools of gore, and still was heard defiance to the death.

---

[1] We will fight to the death for ever and ever and ever.

Now, now the brave defenders in a solid body break
Right through the sod-built barricade, o'er palisade and stake,
And, leaping o'er the trenches, 'mid a storm of shot and shell,
They rushed to liberty or death, still shouting as they fell.

With wild, untutored chivalry, the rebels scorned disgrace,
Oh, never in the annals of the most heroic race
Was bravery recorded more noble or more high,
Than that displayed at Orakau in Rewi's fierce reply—
Ka whawkia tonu! Ake! ake! ake!"

THOMAS BRACKEN.

CHAPTER XII

THE HAU HAUS AND TE KOOTI

NOW at last the war seemed ended. Many chiefs yielded, giving up their lands in token of submission. Sir George Grey kept one quarter of them as punishment for rebellion. The rest he returned.

But meanwhile new trouble had arisen. A wicked and wily native priest had begun to preach a new religion to the people. This new religion was called Hau Hau, because this priest told the people, that if they went into battle shouting Hau Hau, the angel Gabriel would protect them, and they would overcome all their enemies. He also said that the religion of the white people was a religion of lies, and that he had been told in a vision that in the year 1864 all the white people would be swept out of New Zealand.

Although few of the great chiefs followed the Hau Haus, many of the common people did. They did many wild and horrible deeds. Now here, now there, fighting broke out, and so although peace was proclaimed, the land was not really at rest.

The Hau Haus were not gallant and generous foes as the Maoris usually were. They were treacherous and cruel, and their own countrymen often waged war against them. They were driven about from place to place. Many were killed, and many were taken prisoner and sent to the Chatham Islands, which the government had begun to use as a sort of prison-house.

Among the friendly Maoris who helped the British was a young chief called Te Kooti. Now suddenly he was accused of being a traitor. He was seized, and without trial of any kind he was shipped off to the Chatham Islands. There was never any good reason for believing Te Kooti to be false. When Sir George Grey seized Te Rauparaha because he thought he was false, what followed proved that he was right. Only evil followed from the seizing of Te Kooti.

Upon the Chatham Islands there were about three hundred Maori prisoners, most of them Hau Haus. For two years they behaved very well, for they had been told that if they were good they would then be set free and allowed to return home. But the two years came to an end, there was no sign of freedom, and they began to grow restless.

They longed to escape, and one day a ship called the *Rifleman* came to the islands with a cargo of food. Here they saw their chance. Te Kooti was their leader, and quickly he made his plans. Two boatloads of Maoris rowed out to the ship. They swarmed on deck, and almost before any one knew what was happening, the ship was in their hands. All the guards were gagged and bound, only one man being killed in the struggle.

Then Te Kooti took command. He gathered the crew together and ordered them to steer for New Zealand. If they refused, he threatened to shoot them all.

And so the *Rifleman* sailed away, carrying every prisoner and all the guns and ammunition to be found on the islands.

Beside the helmsman stood a Maori armed with gun and sword. Night and day Maori sentries paced the deck. The crew had no choice but to obey their new masters. And so they sailed until they reached Poverty Bay.

Here the Maoris landed, took possession of all the cargo,

and told the crew of the *Rifleman* that they might now go where they liked, as they had no further use for them.

Soon the news of the escape of the Chatham Island prisoners, and of their landing at Poverty Bay reached Wellington, and a force set out to retake the runaways.

But Te Kooti was a warrior. He had plenty of guns and ammunition, and again and again the British troops fell back before him. From his forest fastnesses Te Kooti flung defiance at the foe. But in the wild hills where he had taken refuge there was little food to be had. Soon the provisions taken from the *Rifleman* were all done. Te Kooti and his men were starving.

Then all the savage awoke in them, and they swept like hungry wolves down upon the peaceful settlers of Poverty Bay, and slaughtered them all unresisting in their beds. Men, women, and children, none were spared. With fire and sword they blotted out the settlement, scarce a soul escaping to tell the tale.

A thrill of horror ran through the country when the news was spread. Quickly a force was gathered and sent against the daring chieftain. But he, safe in a fastness perched upon a rock two thousand feet high, with rugged cliffs and wild gorges all around, defied every attempt to take him.

At length, however, with the help of a native chief called Ropata, who had won great renown as a soldier, the pah was one night surrounded.

The besiegers made sure that the next day they would seize their prey. But during the night Te Kooti and his band escaped, sliding down the almost sheer precipice and fleeing to the wilds.

Then in the morning, when it was found that the pah was empty, the chase began and was pitilessly pursued. Many of the Hau Haus were killed, many more were taken prisoner, and they, as soon as they were led before their conquerors, were mercilessly shot, and their bodies thrown over the steep cliffs. Many others died among the lonely mountains, but Te Kooti, wounded, half-starved, weary and desperate, escaped.

With a few faithful followers he wandered for two years a wretched exile. With the price of £5000 upon his head, he was hunted and hounded. Living on fern root, often near death from hunger, he at length gave himself up, was pardoned, and henceforth lived in peace.

All this fighting took place in North Island. In the meantime South Island was at peace, growing daily richer and greater. And in 1871 peace came to North Island too, and since then there have been no more wars.

In 1864 the Parliament had been moved from Auckland to Wellington, Wellington being nearly in the centre of the islands, and so more suitable. In 1868 an Act was passed by which Maori members sat in Parliament as well as white people, and that helped to sweep away many differences. The old days of fighting and misunderstanding are, we hope, gone for ever, and now Maori and Briton live and work side by side. For although of the eighty members of Parliament only four are Maori, every man and woman, over the age of twenty-one, whether Maori or white, has a vote.

In the last thirty-five years many things have happened in New Zealand—things which will be more interesting to you later on. New Zealand has grown and grown, and, in 1907, it was declared no longer a colony but a dominion. Like Canada it is a confederation of self-governing states. It has its own Parliament and Law Courts, yet remains a part of the British Empire.

LIST OF KINGS AND GOVERNORS

Kings of Great Britain and Ireland.	Governors of New Zealand.
Queen Victoria, ... 1837	
	Captain Hobson, . . . 1840
	Lieutenant Shortland, . . 1842
	(temporary)
	Captain Robert Fitzroy, . . 1843
	Captain George Grey, . . 1845
	(Sir George Grey)
	Lieut.-Col. R. H. Wynyard, . 1854
	(temporary)
	Colonel Thomas Gore Browne, 1855
	Sir George Grey, . . . 1861
	Sir George Ferguson Bowen, . 1861
	Sir George Alfred Arney, . . 1873
	(temporary)
	Sir James Ferguson . . . 1873
	Marquess of Normanby, . . 1874
	Chief Justice James Prendergast, 1879
	(temporary)
	Sir Hercules Robinson, . . 1879
	Chief Justice James Prendergast, 1880
	(temporary)
	Sir Arthur Gordon, . . . 1880
	Chief Justice James Prendergast, 1882
	(temporary)
	Sir William Drummond Jervois, 1883
	Earl of Onslow, . . . 1889
	Earl of Glasgow, . . . 1892
	Earl of Ranfurly, . . . 1897
Edward VII., ... 1901	
	Lord Plunket, ... 1904
George V., ... 1910	Lord Islington, . . . 1910